The Wound of the Name

The Wound of the Name

✦

Abdelkébir Khatibi

Translated from the French by Matt Reeck

NORTHWESTERN UNIVERSITY PRESS
EVANSTON, ILLINOIS

Northwestern University Press
www.nupress.northwestern.edu

Chapter 2 was previously published as "Tattoos: Writing in Dots." *PMLA* 137, no. 2 (2002): 295–310. Reprinted with permission.

Support for this publication came in part through the Global Humanities Initiative, which is jointly supported by Northwestern University's Buffett Institute for Global Studies and Kaplan Institute for the Humanities.

Printed in the United States of America

10 9 8 7 6 5 4 3 2 1

ISBN 978-0-8101-4851-2 (paper)
ISBN 978-0-8101-4852-9 (cloth)
ISBN 978-0-8101-4853-6 (ebook)

Cataloging-in-Publication Data are available from the Library of Congress.

Your name is your destiny.

Hindu proverb

CONTENTS

TRANSLATOR'S NOTE

The article "Décolonisation de la sociologie au Maghreb" ("Decolonizing Sociology in the Maghreb"), written by the celebrated Moroccan writer Tahar Ben Jelloun, appeared in the August 1974 edition of *Le Monde diplomatique*. While it is hardly ever cited in scholarly works on Abdelkébir Khatibi, the essay directly pertains to *The Wound of the Name*, published in the same year, as Ben Jelloun relies upon Khatibi's thinking to argue for the importance of decolonizing sociology in North Africa.

Focusing on his native country of Morocco, Ben Jelloun laments the closure in 1969 of the Institut de sociologie (Sociology Institute) in Rabat. The institute had played a crucial role in Khatibi's life. It was there that Khatibi first worked upon returning to Morocco from France. After finishing his PhD in sociology at the Sorbonne (where he was trained by Roland Barthes, among others), Khatibi took up a research position at the Sociology Institute in 1964. Two years later, he became the institute's director. Its eventual shuttering is symbolic in Ben Jelloun's narrative of the challenges facing sociology—and the social sciences generally—in North Africa. Ben Jelloun asks whether a critical reappraisal of knowledge is possible in postcolonial countries since it involves the state's willingness to engage in introspective and self-critical enterprises. He quotes Khatibi to answer this question: no—at least not in the case of Morocco.

Khatibi is the central authority in Ben Jelloun's essay. He speaks of what must happen for sociology to be decolonized. It will need both "scientific independence from the metropole" and a "critical scientific politics based on comparative analysis." Khatibi is sure that anthropology must also be put under the knife. In anthropology's case, the need for revision stems from how that social science is "linked to colonization and imperialism" and so "its theoretical basis is compromised."[1]

Ben Jelloun mentions in passing that Khatibi had recently returned from a sociology conference in Caracas, Venezuela. The conference proved important in the evolution of Khatibi's thinking. A full recapitulation of Khatibi's views on the proceedings was published in the February 1973 issue of the intellectual magazine *Lamalif*. In that issue, the magazine's publisher, Zakya Daoud, interviews Khatibi. Entitled "We Must Attempt a Lasting Double Critique," the interview unveils what would in time become perhaps his most important concept, that of double critique.[2] Double critique is an epistemological method turned simultaneously against colonial European social scientific practices and postcolonial North African epistemological strictures. In *The Wound of the Name*, it is clear that Khatibi is interested in putting into practice a decolonizing sociological and anthropological methodology, yet there remains room for scholars to think at greater length about the particular intervention described in the book.

We know from the book's introduction that Khatibi was interested in writing about forms of North African popular life that had been passed over by Western colonial anthropologists and sociologists and that were being suppressed by the postcolonial state in its turn toward theocracy. The subject matters of the book's five chapters exist under explicit bans or implicit taboos put in place by these two strong pressures that, to Khatibi's mind, unjustly restrict North African self-knowledge: proverbs, tattoos, Cheikh Nafzawi's sex manual *The Perfumed Garden*, calligraphy, and oral storytelling. To be sure, these topics are by no means homogeneous. For instance, they do not belong exclusively to the masses, oral culture, or illiterate society. They are not even exclusively North African. The eclecticism of the book's contents is seemingly, then, an important part of the comparative method that he presents as part of the decolonization of the social sciences.

In the book, these subjects are tethered together not in an overwhelmingly rational, geographical, or disciplinary way but through what Khatibi calls "experimental intersemiotics." The idea is inspired by Roman Jakobson's tripartite division of translation, in which intersemiotics is the transfer of signs from one semiotic system to another—signs, in this case, that go beyond the linguistic.[3] One simple way to think of intersemiotics is through the rubric of book-to-film adaptation, or any adaptation of artwork from one medium to another. Khatibi refers to how signs can drift in and out of different sign systems (he calls it "migrating") and, as they embed in new surroundings, manifest different meanings. But nothing is that simple in Khatibi's imagination.

Conceptualizing the drift of a sign through different sign systems is most easily accomplished through visual and spatial means. Epistemological commitments—such as Khatibi's decolonizing intersemiotics—can be difficult to understand without visuospatial metaphorization. For example, Michel Foucault's books from the 1960s—*Madness and Civilization* (1961), *The Birth of the Clinic* (1963), *The Order of Things* (1966), and *The Archaeology of Knowledge* (1969)—spatialize his epistemological method through the polysemy of the word *field*, which is at once abstract and highly visual and so serves as an effective metaphor. While reading Khatibi, I tend to think of these fields as immense quadrilaterals, cantilevered so as to make for easier viewing into the planes. A linguistic sign gains entry into a field through an enunciation, a new statement, or the first use of the sign in this particular discursive system; a dot appears on the quadrilateral's plane and is soon linked to others, as in network mapping or the stitching together of a constellation's stars with imaginary lines to aid the beginner stargazer. In a discursive formation, each enunciation comes to have its meaning through admixture into the exchanges that define related enunciations.

Tattoos and proverbs, calligraphy and the erotic imagination, and the mirages and majesty of oral storytelling and its narrative fare (fables, fairy tales, allegories, and riddles) are not all of the same sign system. The original sign that circulates through these systems is not conclusively given in this book, but it is suggested through another visuospatial metaphor. In the introduction, Khatibi uses the image of a crystal to articulate the diffusion that links these chapters. A ray of light fed through a crystal refracts in many directions, taking on new life and new colors. Without a doubt, this is the sort of propulsive and dispersive—that is, eccentric—logic that appeals to Khatibi. What the original ray of light would be in this metaphor, however, remains shrouded in mystery, since the suggestion is not that the meaning of calligraphy is transmuted into that of the proverb, or into any of the other sign systems under study. Nothing so banal is taking place. In order to complete this visual metaphorization, the original sign must be seen as something as abstract as the genius of Arab, Arabic, or Islamic culture, which has the paradoxical quality of being at once a single energy source and, inevitably, an origin of multiplicity and difference.

Some have described Khatibi's intersemiotics in wholly nonvisual terms. The scholar David Fieni has argued that Khatibi's intersemiotics is not essentially about the transfer of a sign from one discrete discursive field to another, where it articulates differently. Rather, he argues that the *inter-* in the word *intersemiotics* refers to the location of the Khatibian sign outside of known formations.[4] The intersign refers, then, to the integument of the discursive formation as a whole; this integument and its propensity toward putting enunciations into relation could equally stretch from one discursive formation to another. I have described this potential as akin to the occupation of the vast majority of the universe by dark matter that is undetectable through direct observation.[5] (Dark matter, in this analogy, is the integument of meaning.) So, if we continue along these lines, in the interspace of Khatibi's idea of signification, the sign is articulated against other drifting enunciative moments, as a sense emerges of a more flexible sign, with a more creative or fluid hue to its meaning. Through the notion of a meaningful but somewhat elusive sign is also a good way of approaching these essays. It makes immediate sense in the book's first chapter on proverbs. There, against the colonial anthropologist's desire to regulate language and to fix meaning in a proverb dictionary, against the colonial anthropologist's implicit mission to prove mastery of world cultures to a metropolitan audience, Khatibi suggests a flexibility of meaning within Moroccan proverbs that takes into account aesthetics and the social moment of recitation (which acts as a mobile discursive field). In one of the great phrases of the book, he says that understanding proverbs demands "lazy wisdom" (*sagesse oisive*)—a suspension of Western imperial knowledge's teleological pull in favor of an epistemology that can take place only in slow time.

Khatibi has a reputation as a difficult author. But this reputation is not entirely deserved. For instance, *Plural Maghreb* (1983) is highly accessible and widely popular.[6] If one work deserved the label of difficult, it would be *The Wound of the Name*, which is, in fact, one of his least read works. In general, this reputation comes from the fact that his work never lacks for ideas, and many of these ideas were exceedingly progressive for the context of their initial reception: French-language intellectual circles in France and North Africa in the 1970s and 1980s. So, while the intellectual content of *Plural Maghreb* is presented in a clear fashion and his novels, short stories, poetry, and plays are also usually accessible, we have to deal with style in *The Wound of the Name*, because if we can say confidently that Khatibi knows how to write clear sentences, here he has chosen a different path.

In translation, the translator is presented with a broad but consistent set of choices, but there is no absolute guidance for how to make them. Largely, the type of text affects the translator's calculus: a scientific text is seemingly important for its communication; a literary text is clearly also important for its aesthetics. It would then follow that hewing closely to the communication of a scientific text would be advised, and allowing for greater freedom in a literary text must be allowed for the translator to produce a literary quality resembling the author's. In this text, however, it is clear that Khatibi doesn't abide by some clear-cut, abstract distinction between the scientific and the literary. This is one of the great joys of this book: its intergeneric, or multigeneric, essence. Despite the book's stated social-scientific goals (a decolonization of imperial metropolitan social-scientific method and a freeing from the postcolonial theocratic impulse to ban and deny) and its obvious sociological content, its style is often more in keeping with literary writing: sentence fragments; jumps in argument or plot; rangy and, at times, casually cited intellectual references—all with an ear turned toward the beauty of the phrase rather than some nominal delimitation of communication or content.

Admittedly, all communication involves interpretation. The simplest conversation at home puts the listener in a situation where they are forced to interpret the words heard, and sometimes, because of the essential ambiguity of language or an insufficiently communicated enunciative context (why a person is saying these words at this moment), the listener is challenged to understand the message. This scenario is manifoldly more complicated in sophisticated written texts that are both historical and aesthetic or in other words, whose idiosyncratic style is fundamental to the communication but does not necessarily serve to render transparently a discrete message. As the translator of this subtle yet dense intergeneric and experimental work, I saw my role as both critical and creative, including both interpreting content and rendering aesthetics. At times, I found myself focusing on one over the other, and on second reading, dissatisfaction with the balance led to revisions highlighting the element that had been underrepresented in the previous draft. If, syntactically, Khatibi's sentences in this book "make sense," there are certainly some that I still don't understand and that I would anticipate others having similar difficulty paraphrasing. When confronted with the realization that while I understand the parts, I don't understand the whole of a sentence well enough to present a "clean" English version, I have left things in their nebulous state of appearing to make sense to Khatibi even as readers struggle to access the direction of his thought.

You could argue that he is aspiring to a typical French semiological style, seeing as how he defines the book through experimental intersemiotics, but what would such a style be? That of Roland Barthes? No, Barthes's essays on cultural items (such as in *Mythologies*) are short; it is only his literary essays that have the length and circuitous complexity of Khatibi's essays in this book. So then Julia Kristeva? No, she's much more technical and linguistically oriented. Jacques Derrida? While Derrida and Khatibi were friends, and while they shared important conversations (including those that spurred Derrida to write *Monolingualism of the Other*) and certain stylistic tendencies, Derrida was not a semiotician.[7] *The Wound of the Name* might be situated within the realm of the 1970s French philosophical essay, and its style might have these reference points, but Khatibi's choices are his own.

This book reminds me of a conversation I had several years ago, walking out of the Institut du monde arabe in Paris. Talking about a text by Foucault, my French friend said offhandedly, "No, that would never be seen as publishable today." To my mind, part of the beauty of Khatibi's text, from 1974, is how different it is from today's books—not just on the level of style or content but as an embodiment of the book itself.

This book is the dream of the book—a specific type of book—becoming the book. For that alone (although that's a lot in the end), it deserves more than to be collected in archives. It deserves to be read and reread, to teach us about what writers who continue to take inspiration from Khatibi still strive for: a decolonization of knowledge of North Africa, as well as new social-scientific methodologies that will be better able to represent forms of knowledge that the West has traditionally occluded rather than elucidated.[8]

Figure 1.1. Tunisian Khamsa: Grouper Bones.

Introduction

The Text's Crystal

The dreamed-of book will hover in its most intense moments around several insistent themes: gyratory movement, the wound of the name, a volatile carving, an oblique slap, the point of an argument and the point of a nib. And in this agitation, migratory signs—from one semiotic system (such as tattooing or calligraphy) to another (such as writing)—will retain an interrogative movement, ceaselessly provocative.

Does something like an intersemiotics exist from one semiotic system to another? And, more precisely for us, there is this question: At what moment is knowledge seized by a text, by writing? There is a transference of knowledge to writing in which a hushed emotion and meditative jouissance harmonize in an art of living. There is such an outlay of happy laughter and a scriptural dispersion of the body that the dryness of knowledge capsizes into fiction, without their antagonism ceasing to be virulent. How could one live like this? Or, in other words, how does one establish the power of jouissance? I borrow the phrase "the power of jouissance" from Roland Barthes, to whom our generation owes a more exact—and especially a more jubilant—understanding of the text.

Yet this implies a context where, by a vibratory and almost evanescent asceticism, the subject of the *énoncé* becomes suspended in a voluptuous consciousness of the self, or as Georges Bataille says, a consciousness that "no longer has any object." And because it is sensitive to a critical effacement that pierces and overwhelms it, the subject begins an ascetic practice, renouncing over and over that quality by which ripped desire suggests to the other its vital space—its capacity to breathe, to laugh, and to make love. It is thus violence without hysteria; the subject opens itself to its wound, just as it gives in to every oscillation between nonsense and the pure sign. The orphaned tearing apart of meaning resides there. My joy, my asceticism, resides there. And in this doubling, the concept of the book is intentionally brought into question, both in its closure and its institution.

This movement does not contradict an Orphic slap, such as this Chinese image—absent from the texts that follow—that returns repeatedly to me, bringing with it the decorative motifs that flavor the text. It is said that after having attended a party of "floating cups," Wang Xizhi (301–361) invented his famous calligraphic writing, the most beautiful, reputedly, in all of Chinese art. Let us imagine a rather small, lively river that allows the guests of the emperor to place floating cups full of wine into the river's current. Each would drink, refill the cup, and send it downriver to the next guest—and so on until nightfall. The legend goes that, having returned home completely drunk, Wang Xizhi completed a work of calligraphy so beautiful it would prove inimitable. What of this image? How could such an imperial fury of heavenly bureaucracies justify a power of jouissance? Does such a suspect nostalgia silence history? But it is not an archaic image: the fragmented body—of which we speak freely these days—can be decisive in a work so violent and jubilant as to be able to animate Mallarmé's "pure rhythmic motifs of being."[1] To catch unawares all this agitation of the sign and meaning—this is the project sketched out herein, laid out baldly in its two faces: the ascetic and the Orphic. The project is also positioned in the following way: the texts and the semiotic systems under investigation here all belong to Arab culture, and particularly to the popular culture of Morocco; they are united in the interests of intersemiotic organization. Migratory signs are the gyratory themes of these texts, signs themselves suspended in this mnemonic incandescence that constitutes the Name. This is the reason behind the title of this text, which pivots around the question of its reinscription: its justification (what is a title but "general delivery mail being held for no one"?[2]) is not derived from its empirical use in our analysis of Arab calligraphy (figure 4.2), referring to a royal signature—a tyrannical symbol of power and its appropriation—but rather from its polysemic capacity that opens the pages of the text to a combinatory play and to the fiery veiling of chance.

So the book—a strategic reply to textual memory—and the concept of the book will both be defined as an infinite wound of the Name: in the old French word *blecier* there is the notion of murder; without a doubt, the text is the secretly gyratory place of the mortal activation of our destiny. In the wound, between the wound and the Name, what is at play is essentially the inscription of the Orphic body, shredded but evaporated in its musical being, delivered over to excess but to an excess veiling itself in a cruel reconciliation with nature. Never will any alibi be able to delimit the search for identity (here, the Name)[3] within a simple mirroring of the self and its intimate theater; never will knowledge be able to claim to end in theory the infinity of the text. If the title of a text has any reason for its selection, it is as the punctual effect of the propagation of meaning and its disorder, which writing scans and consumes. And the "author" never knows whether their text has realized a stroke of genius or its opposite.

It's time, then, to leave behind the Hindu proverb "Your name is your destiny" and no longer consider identity as a divine fatality fixed at a center and origin, but put the Name in play according to the crystal of the text: this mirroring of the self transforming, recombining in the riffling of meaning. Your

Name is your destiny, like the crystalline index of an infinite wound to the Orphic text, because no text can easily dismiss the mythic work that animates and traverses it. And in this sense, the science of the text is hardly capable of residing (at the price of what blindness!) in the depths of this mythic work of writing, and when it has to change paths, the science of the text is forced into blind formalism. No doubt, to reconstruct the text in the manner of a Russian doll—by unpacking and packing structural unities—incites a certain epistemological pleasure. Reduced to this show of legerdemain, the enigmas of the text disappear in the illusion of a logical, classificatory infinity.

One can always attempt a more subtle science of language, likely to unknot the formalist activity of our era, by putting a finger on a scientific and critical semiotics of the text and its own laws.[4] I will retain several themes of this form of questioning, in particular the notion of intertextuality. Meanwhile, the attention given to Arab culture and its theories of the sign brings us back with yet more appreciation to the work of Jacques Derrida, although in no way do I pretend to treat the entire breadth of his philosophy here. One crucial argument in his work motivates me: how the metaphysics of the sign, in returning to a Western logocentric tyranny, is hidden from itself while hiding the intelligibility of other cultures. All critical writing can thus only be a heliotropic tearing of the historical being, erasing, through its interrogation, the limits of that tyranny: center, origin, the oppositions of signifier and signified and of intelligible and sensible. It will be a monumental critique through which the concepts of being and nonbeing will be exceeded. At the threshold of this renunciation of the self, a theoretical pause intervenes, and, following the example of Derrida, we can ask ourselves, "Are we the Occident or the Orient?" Unifying this vacillating double identity makes the text an orphaned being, a being of exile. It is in the interval, itself nomadic, of such an identity that destiny finds and wounds itself. "Are we the Occident or the Orient?" This is what that means: in the knowledge of the text, its gem of many facets, particularly here in relation to the divine body as *intersign*, there is a place where the power of jouissance changes in color as if a poison were approaching. An intersign is a mark, an index, or as the dictionary tells us, a "mysterious relation between two things." For us, it is a blood crystal with many facets and a regular tip, whose glassy, fragile iridescence wounds the body and the Name while reinscribing in a different fashion the crystalline symmetry of identity and difference. From the first definition to the second, it is the question of the sign in its full extent that is at stake; from a positivist semiotics to a transversal intersemiotics, it is again the concept of writing that must be invested in the body by placing it as a challenge against the Qur'an and the Arabic language.

In fact, the semiotic systems presented here exist chiefly in relation to Islam and its fundamental semiotics, as a system that either constitutes a veiled, masked propagation of the divine intersign (calligraphy); develops in the interstice of the trace suppressed by Islam (tattooing as the arche-writing of the empty sign); is based upon an oral semiotics, no doubt determined by the text of the Qur'an but whose formal structure goes back to the primitive Story (proverbs and fairy tales); or, finally, bears directly upon the erotic semiotics of a written text, *The Perfumed Garden*. Each arising from what we call popular culture, these semiotic systems reverberate in the Islamic context like a cross holding, a fiery mirroring of the sign instituted by the Qur'an—"a clear word" revealed to Muhammad as a supreme sign of life, death, and the Very Great Violence.[5]

The Qur'an owes its extreme originality to how it defines itself as a radical theory of the sign, of the Word, and of Writing; *al-qur'ân*—the reading, parsing, and recitation of the revealed sign. What we mean by Gabriel's command to Muhammad to read and to repeat the Name of Allah by "opening his chest" is exactly the theory of the breath that passes through the body (in the exact sense that the Qur'an descends into the body), splits it, and folds it into distinct signs so that the believer experiences these fibers as so many crystalline leaves of the text. The prophetic intersign is a breath, an ecstatic discourse, whose plasticity is governed by, accounted for, and veiled and unveiled in the body: "Do not follow blindly what you do not understand: ears, eyes, and heart, you will have to speak for them all."[6] Allah holds in his breast the interpretation of signs and, at the same time, affirms the clarity of his message. Thus, the Qur'an marks the sign in its double face of veiling and unveiling. A hidden god, Allah directs the order of the Unknowable, but he lavishes visible, audible, and tactile—in short, readable—signs upon humankind and the universe. In this relation between God and humankind, the Prophet is not considered the governor of interpretation; he is a simple transmitter, there to give people a "clear warning."[7]

How could humankind—this sign created out of a "drop of sperm"—seize this gesture of presence and absence, if not in the middle of the greatest solitude? Allah is not a god who loves, as in Christianity: he demands from the believer a complete *submission* to the Qur'an. This violent submission to the text will condition the entire status of writing as a body, as a divine intersign. And we know, moreover, what Allah promises to the nonbeliever: they will be turned into an animal, turned into a mineral, left forever in hell, this "Hated Future"; he promises a "rupture of the ears," an "uncircumcised heart." It's Allah who holds fate in his hands, and because the nonbeliever turns their back on the "clear word," Allah will turn their face to the eternal fire.

This divine envelopment of the body is admirably recounted in the allegory of the companions of the cave, plunged into silence for three hundred years: "We sealed their ears with silence in the cave for years."[8] There is a state between sleeping and wakefulness, during which, projected to the center of the cave, the body is reflected to the right and left of the cave through the rotation of the sun. It is thus a place of suspension, of sheltering within the limits of the day and of the night. In waking, the sleepers find again the pulsation of time and recover their senses. What does this waking mean? This allegorical setting defines the Qur'anic theory of the sign, divided between a nocturnal identity marking humankind without God as blind, dumb, and lost, and an illuminated identity coming from the tree of the "good word." It is said, "Allah made the night and the day as two signs, and he darkened the sign of the night and brightened the sign of the day."[9]

This opposition of diurnal and nocturnal determines the status of Arabic, which Allah chose over all "barbarian" languages to make clear the signs of his Word: "We have made the signs clear for those who have knowledge."[10] A strategic intelligibility enters into conflict with the symbolic and parabolic discourse of the Qur'an. From this, the two principal movements that excavate the logocentric closure of Islam become evident: on the one hand, the Rational Word (*nut'q*) replicated without deviation by theologians, philosophers, jurists, and commentators; on the other, the text's infinite meaning adored by prophets, mystics, and poets. Yet it is in an interstitial space where the calligraphic trace opens as a sacred celebration of the sign. Far from being a simple graphic supplement to the word, the calligraphic trace is a composition inside the text, a crystalline production of the linguistic body itself.

The calligraphic letter as divine trace invades all decorative Islamic arts; ceaselessly vying against the void, it carves out space while inhabiting an absolute interior, an absolute interior that allows logography to cover, more or less explicitly, *other* semiotic systems, like tattooing.

The semiotic systems that arose for the most part before Islam are thus suppressed and emptied of their symbolic charge. But as in the language of dreams, these deformed hieroglyphs rip through our imagination and imprint in the body and in the unconscious the gesture of an elastic separation, requiring, in order to be read, a true divestment of logocentric tyranny. How are we to read these torn objects? How are we to pierce and collapse logocentric closure?

To offer such a glimpse of the Arab semiotics of popular culture will require us to attempt in time analyses of many different semiotic systems: fairy tales and proverbs, calligraphy and tattooing, and finally, the erotic text of Nafzawi. Why have I specifically chosen these systems, whose allure seems so fragmentary?

My analyses are organized according to two themes. The first is that all these semiotic systems are a translation of the body and its jouissance: from the trace of the tattoo to incestuous passion (shown here by the story "The Talking Bird"), there is the deployment of euphoric writing. The economy of the text and of pleasure is found here.

The second theme deals with a transversal intersemiotics, whereby knowledge is time and again torn, folded, and caught unawares by textual necessity. It is an intersemiotics along three axes:

1. A graphic semiotics (tattooing, calligraphy), understood in its symbolic density. In the case of tattooing, the empty sign

(anaphora) reproduces a suppressed arche-writing; in the case of calligraphy, it deals with an over-determined mirroring of the linguistic code.

2. A rhetoric of lovemaking, called "the art of the bed chamber" by the ancient Chinese. I have chosen *The Perfumed Garden* because it remains principally oral, in the manner of *One Thousand and One Nights*. Thus, it is situated between learned and popular culture.
3. An oral semiotics (fairy tale, proverb), which will help us determine the relation of voice to myth.

Interest in these semiotic systems would be futile if it did not bring up, at the level of writing, the originality of cultures and, more importantly, the relation of the text to the historical being; without this, it would remain akin to the nostalgic pleasure that certain disillusioned diplomats experience in arranging flower bouquets or Zen gardens or learning how to shoot arrows while timing the breath. The retranslation of popular semiotics forces us to relinquish such nostalgia. To listen to popular culture is a strong ideological intervention that suffuses and contaminates every decision of speech. To write is thus to open—in the body that speaks—the process of historical meaning, by which a class war also takes places *within* the text.

The subject draws to itself the exteriority that creates it—and that will dissolve it.

January 1973

Chapter 1

Paremiological Discourse

1. The Body: A Constellation of Proverbs

To remember proverbs, some people use a mnemonic device, mapping them onto the body. There is nothing astonishing in this economy of language. To cover the body with a symbolically encoded space is an active part of Moroccan popular culture, which encompasses medicine, divination, and enchantment. It's a culture that requires ascetism and an attentive, thoughtful listening. The body is the concentric place where the word begins, where it begins again. In its clever way, the proverb speaks of this gyratory movement; let's be wary of systems that exclude its mention.

So I asked a friend which proverbs about the body he knew, using the mnemonic device. He recounted forty-eight. These constitute our corpus (see the annexes).

This topographic structure isn't arbitrary (recall how *corpus* means *corporeality* before all else). Corpus and corporeality: one is found and founded in the other. This is where ethnographic discourse fails. Face to face with the literature of proverbs, anthropology proceeds with tabulation (but where does this list end? in which space is it enclosed?) and classification (classify discourse through what? a particular logic? which? a code? which? a social class?). So here too we meet with anthropology's prudery (which is false and perverse): the taboo veils the "pornograms" of the literature of proverbs.[1] This taboo must be lifted to allow the culture in question to speak. Anthropology tends to erase difference (cultural or otherwise) without speaking about its subject position vis-à-vis the Other.

While inspired by specific languages (linguistics, anthropology, sociology) and by popular culture (in its Moroccan form), the brief analysis that follows must be approached on its own terms, movements, and gestures. Its goal is to discombobulate the conceptual body in relation to the "true" body that speaks through this constellation of proverbs.

More than just for methodological reasons, our corpus is constituted of a corporeality that is neither feminine nor masculine, or rather it is both at once, a type of (non-Platonic) hermaphrodite that we must try to approach in its irreducible singularity and difference.

Motif. — We know that mnemonic devices are used universally in oral cultures. In Morocco, we used to learn poems that contained medical formulae by rote: syphilis was first treated by several parables, with the medical object coming *afterward.*

To make up for the lack of calligraphy, memory organizes, cordons off space into poems and proverbs: a veritable geography transcribed in proverbs is the basis of the Bedouin's mastery over the desert. Outfitted in this way, they know the route. And what do they do while traveling over the sand, if not trace their own writing out in this empty form, to the rhythm of the mark written in midair?

Likewise, the Bedouin erases with a hand their games and sand writing (just as the child erases words from the Qur᾿anic chalkboard), as if the desert (and the child's act of erasure) suspended the *completion* of meaning: no more writing, no more anything. And if the hyena wanders across the Bedouin's path and a violent confrontation ensues, it's a muted and harmless violence. Let's say that the Bedouin smashes in the hyena's head (with a godly word). The Bedouin's wife will serve its brain to "tie down" the men and control their desires. The talisman will close the system, then change it.

Likewise, the *rammâlûn,* and their magical lines dug into the sands of western Sudan.[2] This is an anomalistic, gyratory gesture intended to create signs that will be swallowed immediately into the void. Heraclitus (a man the likes of which we'll never see again) said, "The hand that writes goes right and then in spirals. This path is one and the same."[3] This path is that of desire. Arab calligraphers know it; like a wink, so often cited in the Qur᾿an (which writes of a violent desire that can never be appeased),[4] the formation of a letter captures the quickness of life. Initially, the formation of consonants was done in *black,* and the vocalization (the base of Semitic musical semantics) in *red.*[5] Add diacritical marks and read the text as a fugue. It's possible to think of calligraphy as a refined form of the intersemiotic.

It's by this violence, sung by the ends of the fingers, that the (Arabic) letter is a letter doubly purloined,[6] disappearing into space (the written) and time (the melodic) by a wink's glint.

The graphic projection circle of the twenty-eight consonants (see figure 1.2) is the image that justifies this art. The old mnemonic devices are used for etching the alphabet into the child's mind (in Qur᾿an school). The circle contains the twenty-eight consonants, each on its own merit, and *alif* and *lâm* span its width. The contiguousness of the two letters, as has been said, remains truly mysterious. We can imagine that, as though in overview, this is where the doxological law resides, traverses the entire circle, and, at the same time, opens it and projects it into the void.

Figure 1.2. Arabic Consonant Circle. Calligram by Muhammed Lemaalmine.

2. Paremiological Discourse

Two Circles

We wash our faces, hands, forearms up to the elbows; we rub our heads with our wetted right hands; then we wash our feet. This is how Muslims ease into prayer. Water is the first separation; the opposition of pure/impure hierarchizes the body, the parts of the body (each place will have its *lack*); and, in this discourse full of desire, the prayer admits to an impossible speech; it finishes, we know, by the circular game of the rosary (the hand releases a fanciful aggressiveness into the rosary), by murmuring, and by the psalmody whose whispered rhythm is the only thing we can make out. This is how the body of the Prophet Muhammad unfolds, in the breath of *chaj'* (rhymed prose)—the very Prophet who once said that the poet is a trickster. *Who* listens? The fiat of prophetic discourse is already a historical code. And if we asked our Prophet about what he thinks of our indiscretion, he would undoubtedly say, "Whosoever of you sees an evil, let him change it with his hand; and if he is not able to do so, then let him change it with his tongue; and if he is not able to do so, then with his heart."[7]

The psalmody isn't a vertical ascension, as mystics would have us believe; rather it's a dispersion, a propagation of the body (discourse is here a body, always a body), an illusory propagation disguised at its highest point in the pedagogical detachment of the believer. More precisely, it's an illusion of the quest for the impossible itself. We must see this demonstrative gesture (and what does it point to but the void?), this hand, this water that separates, this prayer as exercises for reconciling the violent gap between us and our desires. This is the source, it seems to us, of our Muslim habit (during prayer) of touching the forehead to the ground. And we know that this element (the ground) is the tomb of signs, the theoretical limit of our most foolish, most baroque systems; it is the intimate rotting of our senses. To die is no doubt to speak in another way. Our proverb (proverb 24 in the annexes) says to the cadaver: Yuk![8]

The *doxological* body is to be read like an intersemiotic score: time, space, and knowledge create a circular hierarchy. The center is a burnished fixation, a fantasy of the void. The officiant gives up his body to be the body of the other. We allow him to believe that this illusion is divine but only while knowing that such an appropriation of the body risks making God disappear.[9] That is where the hairline crack of desire resides. That is also where our difference from the reciter resides: between the divine breath and the rotting of desire, we choose the hilarious laughter (of the proverb), which itself *knows*.

The *paremiological* body makes up a concentric circle in relation to the other circle, a traced-out, sketched-in circle: the talisman is often a group of proverbs, by which we're protected against the paralysis of signs, that mortal illness. But this circle is in some ways made banal, flattened. And it's so modest as well! The proverb lends to the mystic some of its tics and psalmodic quavering, and they reduce all of it to a purr, a satirical debauchery. With a theater of movement, they fake the doxological body but without hysteria: there's the farcical proverb as well as the pornographic proverb. That's why the proverb (this is another lesson in Heraclitean wisdom) is a tricky tautology. Will we ever know enough about this touching, this tact, this ever-so-modest measure? It's this irony that holds firm in us, this confounding of signs that are so small: the proverb undresses the doxological body. At worst, I suspect the mystic of impiety. The popular proverb puts it this way: "The wise man laughs only while trembling."[10]

3. The Proverb as an Empty Form

> Go away, fly, I'm pregnant with my Lord.[11]

Stripped of its cultural references (conventional signifiers), this Moroccan proverb has nothing to say. That's where its riddle begins. It's an empty form, whose rhythmic movement caresses our ears. Grasping this first paradox is important for appreciating paremiological discourse.

For the moment, then, we must set aside the social order that envelops proverbs in a ritual, repetitive time, which is that of conversation. Its function at this level isn't to decode the "real" by a simple metaphorical mechanism or by a parabolic amplification; it's to obstinately work *against* the word.

With proverbs, the rite brings into the conversation a full system—that is, a repetitive time, a truncated space, and a tautological knowledge, since the signified is assumed to be known by the interlocuters. The proverb serves as a pretext for the emptying of meaning. This is the cause of all errors of interpretation. Let's think of the proverb not as a pretext for ritual but as a text, albeit composed of a single sentence.

Linguists have generally classified proverbs with ready-made utterances, a rubric that emphasizes their value as social speech. John Lyons writes,

> From a strictly grammatical point of view such utterances are not profitably regarded as sentences. . . . Their internal structure, unlike that of genuine sentences, is not accounted for by means of rules which specify the permissible combinations of words. However, in a total description of the language, which brings together the phonological and the grammatical analysis, they might be classified as (grammatically unstructured) sentences, since they bear the same intonation contour as sentences generated by the grammar. Apart from this fact, they are to be accounted for simply by listing them in the dictionary with an indication of the situations in which they are used and their meaning.[12]

Is the proverb a true or false sentence? The question is secondary, insomuch as this presumed falseness turns our attention from the proverb's rhetorical refinement. A. J. Greimas brought the particularities of such a system to light by insisting on the necessary archaism of its grammatical composition; on its rhythmic, binary structure; and on its anti-historical temporality, comparable in this regard to myths and dreams. He contrasts proverbs, with their connotational (and figurative) meaning, to sayings, which have no connotation.[13] Other distinctions are important as well. The proverb seems to be akin to the poem in its rhythmic scansion, through which is born a certain power: precision; a compact, powerful image (which is also often violent); and rhetorical figuration. Like all forms of literary discourse, it obeys the laws of analogy, in particular, metaphor and metonymy. But the proverb is also unlike the poem: the énoncé of the proverb is minimal, almost closed, but capable of a brief expansion, while the poem is an operation, a transformation of several énoncés, of multiple texts. The proverb plays at neutralizing intertextuality, which complicates considerably its enigma and the question of the *place* of its elocution.

The proverb is a small, quasi-closed, and stubborn system whose function is to fight against the transitoriness of spoken language. These distinctive features don't turn it into the discourse of the enigma (or riddle) or that of the anagram, or that of the Saussurian anaphone either.[14] The riddle has its rules; it's enough to know them to posit the boundaries of the system: a riddle always bites its tail, always leads to more puzzlement.

E. K. Maranda tells us the following:

> Proverbs are "images" or *signantes* derived from the context that furnishes *signata*, and so riddles are *signantes* in which we must find *signata*. Their only real difference rests then in the fact that the *signatum* of a proverb cannot be—and, ordinarily, isn't—named and labeled as clearly as that of the riddle's image.[15]

This is a difference that supposes the anteriority of the signified (which simplifies the internal relation of the sign), as if the signifying production and its transformation didn't change *everything* about the sign.

The discourse of riddles, the interplay between two or more partners, brings about its closure (that of the text) through its initial strategy and the arbitrariness of its end. Metaphorically, the space of the riddle's discourse is a rosary whose each and every bead touches the next to take its place. Each time, there is an occupied place.[16]

4. The Proverb: Symmetrical Organization

Linguistically, the proverb has a binary rhythmic structure.[17] The small corpus that we're going to study doesn't escape this rule (see the annexes): a binary structure that can be separated (in most cases) into a four-part énoncé.[18] Likewise, we can identify three typical structures.

1. *Simple structure*: composed of two words and a unique metaphor, often formed by assonance:

ʿaynak	mîzânak
tes yeux	sont ta balance
your eyes	*weigh things out*

bḥâl chʿar	fi-l'jîna
comme des cheveux[19]	dans la pâte
like hairs	*in pasta*

Remark. It's true that we could call the first example a proverb, and the second example a saying—or we could call both sayings. But dialectal Arabic assimilates them into the same linguistic system, where the lexical distinction between proverbs and sayings no longer exists.

2. *Compound structure*: an énoncé whose two units are sentences held in balance, whether or not the proverb's "head" and "tail" rhyme and whether or not there's assonance:

illa hzal kûl ar-râs
oula sman kûl ar-râs

s'il (sujet neutre) maigrit mange-lui la tête
s'il grossit mange-lui la tête

if it's skinny eat its head
if it's fat still eat its head

Remark. This proverb is born of a rigorously Aristotelian analogy but an analogy flattened to the point of emptiness. This is an example of the proverb's bricolage.

3. *Complex structure*: a three-part énoncé that is a simple expansion of the binary structure. This amplifying process ironizes meaning *per se*; it's an overvalorization written onto a *false* (flat) paradigmatic richness:

Chʿand al-qarʿa ma tarʿâ
ghîr al-machtʾa ou khyûtʾ rashâ?

De quoi peut s'occuper une chauve
sinon de son peigne et de ses cheveux?

What would a bald woman worry about
if not her comb and her hair?[20]

5. Thematic Variations

Now we ask the reader to read the entire proverb corpus (found in the annex).

Violence

In our corpus, there's an explicitly cannibalistic violence born of madcap sadism: a head stuck in a beehive; gouged-out eyes; heads cut off in a single blow (the very thing of epics); a punched throat. . . . The proverb mumbles sentence-shouts, onomatopoetic phrases, a slightly giddy discourse. It's the maddest form of pent violence; it's drunken pleasure and leaping jouissance. (See proverbs 3 and 4, but the analysis that follows has to do with proverb 3.)

Ar-râs bla nachwâ?	Qtʾiʿû ḥlâl.
Tête morose?	La trancher est permis.
Headache?	*Cutting it off is halal.*

The word *nachwâ* means drunkenness. Due to the presence of this excess, the proverb doesn't need to rhyme. It covers the doxological body with a double movement: In the proverb's first unit, the taboo on crazy jouissance is lifted (although the *wâw* of the *nachwâ* is considered by Arab mystics to be a symbol of the intellect). The second movement undercuts the religious lexicon; because it means "licit," the word *ḥlâl* can take the place of rhyme. The violence is lightly decentered, the "breath" is taken out of the proverb—not just through the failure of its expected musicality but also through its subversion of Arabic's "authoritarian dialectic."[21] Here, rhyme would have constituted an economic surplus; as is, the proverb gives rise to hilarious laughter. Its greatest trick is to knot, then unknot, binary semantic oppositions according to a slight back-and-forth expansion in each segment's final vowels. In one sense, the proverb deflates the spoken word; the rite then becomes necessary for language's social functioning. When I say a proverb, it's certainly not an innocent ex post facto reference used to stop discursive violence; it's rather a signal to my interlocuter that they can't control my body like that. The interlacing of the proverb requires ritual time, the pause of pleasure, and the movement of meaning almost in motion.

Like a veil being pared back, this proverb shucks off a double taboo: that of the sacred doxological body and that of the proverb's musical semantics, which will be embodied in an alternation and an oblique movement. The technique is to constrict then loosen the rhythm by a calculated surprise in an irreverent strabismus, hiccup, or trembling: a burst of laughter! And, to be sure, this proverb doesn't undercut its semantic richness and melodic possibilities; instead, it uses them so skillfully, or, better said, with such a loving excess that the listener must truly take pleasure first before trying to understand, even just a little. Listening to proverbs demands the lazy wisdom of slow time.

A narcissistic image in one proverb and debauched rhetoric in another: that's the mobility of famous Mexican jumping beans. When the anthropologist or the linguist tells us that the literature of proverbs is of little interest because its signification is linked to a sociocultural context, what are we to say? If there's an irreducible difference, if there's exogamy, it can be located only in language in the combinatorial space beyond classificatory knowledge. For these two sciences (I would have liked to use a different word), the proverb is a lesson in modesty.

The poet takes pleasure in the rhyming dictionary, a favored possession, a perversion when feeling blue, as though the text closes in on itself when there's rhyme and a drumbeat. Rhyme is an insistent signature, a fetishized attribute, whereas the proverb floats in utter anonymity. The trace that rhyme leaves is disseminated in the text itself, a signifying form of communal property, of language. Mallarmé speaks of the "words of the tribe."[22] If there's tribalism, we need to look for its murky internal semiotics in the irony of the proverb's oppositional violence. Why should we stubbornly search for social structures in hallucinatory ideologies?

A proverb that is rhymed in one region may simply contain assonance in another, or neither rhyme nor assonance in a third—and so on and so forth to infinity. It's not that a proverb's variants are based principally on a cultural code but rather that, in the economy of the proverb, the decentering of signs constitutes dispossession.

Arab culture is just like that! Oral literature is also the archaeology of original knowledge. And from here the fiat of the angel Gabriel to Muhammad is born: "Read."[23] While this inaugurates an undeniably authoritarian dialectic, the merit of Arab culture is to have given an admirable text—the Qur'an—before retroactively creating its God. Then, after the heights of classical knowledge, the *maqâmât*, a degraded form of popular literature, appeared. That novelistic and anecdotal form is an appropriated style of storytelling, created by a caste of scribes for the pleasure of kings: rhyme proclaims a true state of exception, and the proverb becomes the pretext for a semantic economy in the service of money. By citing proverb 6, we can make plainly obvious our self-contradictions: "O rich bald man, let me kiss your pasty pate." But the kiss isn't a link between money and disease-like baldness; it's a huge clap of laughter. The economy of proverbs—as it must be—is an autarkic economy. All parts of the system are involved at once.

The archaeology of knowledge is multiple; it's also uncontestably a part of popular culture. Will we remain condemned to forget forever these traces of our historical being? Western culture is just like that! Linguists and psychoanalysts often forget that mysticism (popular or elitist) has already given a revolutionary language to the spoken word. Why should we fixate on the archaeology of childhood and then, by an abuse of theory, put to sleep historical time in the name of unconscious meaning?[24]

The Art of the Bagatelle

We have unlearned to speak in proverbs. In their place, we have substituted a group of somewhat idiotic stereotypes whose general rhetoric is realized anew "day and night" (which is the name of a café franchise) in newspapers, on the radio, and on TV. This imperial discourse wipes everything out, ruining the imagination and its forms. Its function is to classify, to locate us within institutions and social structures. But this is not the consummation of a discourse that describes us; it's the violence of febrile and hilarious self-destruction, in such a way that we grant desire's compromised power to our tension and that our little intimate drama takes flight in likenesses and mirrors while we practice corporal asceticism. In the breath, the whole enunciation process is at play. Rhetorical consciousness exists between the real and the possible.

Since I'm a member of a proverb culture, I'm able to invent poetic proverbs. No one ever asks me to explain, but this isn't because the meaning is clear to all (that's a mistake of anthropological discourse) but because the art of the bagatelle (including the proverb) is a combinatorics of consummation founded—as is proper—on the empire of the illusion and representation. Always representation. Even when we displace the place of its making, discourse is always representation.

How is rhetoric put into action while inventing a proverb? By suspending the automation of repetition (in a non-Freudian sense) through the play of tropes and figurative language, a form of play that takes place in the language of proverbs: triliteralism sets the consonants, the dialectic syntax, and it's this trivocalism that makes the consonant field dynamic—to learn to speak or to vocalize (the child at Qur'an school recites and learns to write Qur'anic calligraphy) is to tie oneself to an ascetism of desire, to learn to speak into being the desire for the other (whether or not doxological), to burrow into the violent overdetermination of musical semantics.

If my body is periphrastic, I will use a series of *mûzâwaqât* figures (literally, *decoration*; in French, it's a metaphor for coupling), principally simple or compound paronomasia. By this figuration, my discourse is dependent; it becomes the other through a simple verbal interlacing, a purr of pleasure. Ideally, it will be a proverbial creation for my kin as well as for my kith, the entire tribe. If there's an incestuous complication, it must be suspended in an interstitial wink springing from the word.

But if I'm around a bunch of boys, I'll speak in spoonerisms and metaplasms that alter the radical consonants in Arabic but that assure the androgynous pleasure of my body. Herein metaplastic theory finds its reason for being, its art of living. Because I like the number three and three-part rhythms (as dear to Bedouins as to Proust: what a strange conjunction!), I will mime the donkey's intersemiotic braying:

> chhîq nhîq ḥzîq
> braiement braiement pet
> *bray bray fart*

Here, the transcription system is born of spoonerism.

And we know that in Morocco there's this one as well: "When a boy is forced to swallow a donkey's tongue and maybe its ears, how will enough of its brain be left for working or doing anything else for that matter?"

This is how proverbs work. A proverb plays out on two levels. First, it perverts rhetoric through lexical excess (with proverbs, there's no end to words), but this is a doubled, interior figurative play set up in the rigging of a flat semantic patina, which carries the proverb to the borders of meaninglessness. Take proverb 14: "However high your eyes might rise, they're still beneath your eyelashes" (I'm translating from the Arabic). The first unit has a four-part rhyme, the same broad rhyme, which is symbolically charged: *alif-lâm* is a Qur'anic riddle. The second unit is prosaic, maliciously prosaic; assonance wears away, and the rest is flat, banal, sliding into a comic decrescendo.

Nietzsche, who knew this music only too well, writes, "The principal sensorial task seems to me to be perceiving the form, resting on a mirror. Space and time are only *measured* things, measured by a rhythm."[25]

One of the secrets of the proverb is to generalize pleasure: a brief énoncé mobilizes rhetorical play and musical semantics at the same time (which is no small feat). The jubilation of the auditor comes from the autarkic economy that is ready to explode in a potlatch. According to Freud, pleasure is similarly suspended between autarky and potlatches, between meaningfulness and meaninglessness.

To Translate

Roman Jakobson wondered, "Translator of what messages? Betrayer of what values?" That was after he noted that "poetry by definition is untranslatable. Only creative transposition is possible: either intralingual transposition . . . or interlingual transposition . . . , or finally intersemiotic transposition."[26] What did he mean? When it comes to translating proverbs, we're used to giving a behind-the-scenes look at the work of translation and not mentioning how proverbs work. We give the translation along with the original meaning, followed by brief commentary that tells you that the proverb is used on such and such an occasion, which makes it meaningful and justifies its existence as such. These are precautions that help the translator avoid nonsense: something has to be communicated, after all. . . . But between nonsense and the quest for pure language,[27] there remains the entire task of translation. For sure, translation is a literary transposition but a transposition that demands intense theoretical effort. What a strange desire! To translate is to tempt self-destruction in the violent gap between two languages.

When we translate proverb 15 as follows, what do we really do? "The days/having little cheeks comeandgo the days/having kids." In relation to the original, the transposed text loses its two-part integrity, that is, its "head" and "tail." The first gesture is to attenuate expressivity to try to communicate something. So I chose a literal transposition that is subverted in two moments: first, I glued together the two verbs (which no longer rhyme) to bring into balance the two segments, then I added two slashes, one between "days" and "having little cheeks" and the other between "days" and "having kids."[28] The semantic castration is strongly marked, and so the proverb retains its riddle-like element (at least, I hope) and its difference. To translate is to reveal the rigging of the violent gap.

Refrain

The proverb's refrain is founded on a nonchalant indeterminacy: a light and ironic touch, an implosive-explosive movement of rhythm and syntax. Take, for example, the two rhymed words *mâ* and *jamjamâ* of proverb 5, "What's seared into the mind can never be erased." The dialectal word *jamjamâ* indicates the skull (in written Arabic, *jumjumâ* is also a wooden bowl and a well dug in saline soil). The meaning of *mâ* runs the gamut from trickling water to something distantly related, sperm.[29] Between these two rhymed words there are five phonemes: an economic reduction that sets up the relation between syntax and rhythm and that can only faintly disrupt the oppressive totality.[30]

In the past, we tattooed the skull so that the dead person would remain property, a written being. This is just how the proverb works; it closes the field of orality with the presence of the sign: the written being alone can resist the cosmic order. But it's a partial, airy presence in the rhythmic act of disappearance. It's not that the intelligible and the sensible fall into ruin in this rhetoric; rather, it's that the metaphor retains its hollow form, its empty enunciation, while floating.

And it's because rhyme exiles knowledge to a form of orality that is always threatened, always at risk of disappearing, that Claude Lévi-Strauss proposes to us an even more opaque riddle: "Music [is] the supreme mystery of the science of man, a mystery that all the various disciplines come up against and which holds the key to their progress."[31]

Madness

Normally, we get to the other side of the river by swimming or in a boat. Proverb 9 picks up on this imagery: "With a head full of brimstone, we conquer the river." Madness is a monumental geography, and space is the very limitlessness of such spoken words.

That's why in the Moroccan countryside there's a certain way of curing mental illness: the insane person is buried, just as butter and other provisions are buried. The person is kept there for a day or two, without food and almost naked. The insane person is reborn or dies, as is fitting.

The proverb's derision is to insinuate that what is possible is akin to madness and that the "real" is only a symbol, an opening into madness that lives in us. Madness is a fiction divided by speech: on the one hand, there's epic, violently cosmic space; on the other, there's deflated, crooked time. The énoncé of the proverb above is a smooth, unattributed simplification; only inversion—more modest than modesty itself—can "cook" rhetoric.

By pushing and prodding, we can bypass the space of parabolic discourse and of the doxological body. Nietzsche's "wild wisdom" relies on having exploded a similar parabolic discourse to the point of disorienting knowledge and derisively undermining the very notion of the human as a sign.[32] To give life to the body is to destroy through it the fixed limits of its symbolization.

Laughter

What is laughter? Al-Jahiz tells us that laughter has three functions: *logical*, since laughter is the demonstration of an argument; *moral*, since laughter *is produced* from utility, as a law of vital economy; and *erotic*, since laughter unknots the body and corrects our penchant for crying, which, al-Jahiz says, risks blinding us.[33] Laughter is part of a divine order: the religious conscience consists of giving moral health to each of our limbs, of controlling their disorder under God's watch through joyous words. However, doxological laughter is a pallid laughter. It's repressive, and it divides and hierarchizes the limbs and the senses into the pure and the impure. The body is a table of values whose center is elsewhere; laughter constitutes its floating trace, which conjures disorder. The moral principle of laughter shakes in fear of madness. The proverb respects this principle but muddies its realization.

The proverb's kiss is Judas's kiss. To safeguard God's omnipresence, the proverb (even when naughty) suspends it through archaic redundancy: synecdoche, for example, is childhood's favorite trope. It's the unfurling of our primitive fantasies: the servant's lips as large as an amphora, arms as big as the mouth. It's the same refrain of tousled cruelty, played within a gyratory mode, like that of a top. The proverb's highest art is to grate rhetoric that's easy and flat.

We understand Georges Bataille better while meditating on the Nietzschean parable and while transforming knowledge through a simple excitation—laughter: "I laugh naively, *divinely*. I don't laugh when I'm sad, and when I laugh, I'm truly happy."[34]

The Pornographic Proverb

Like Lévi-Strauss, we can imagine a pornographic triangle that obeys the categories of the raw, the cooked, and the rotten. To make this correspondence more systematic (and more delirious), we can count all the tropes by which sex "is cooked." The Berber woman's vagina, we're told, is salty, whereas the Fez woman's vagina is sugary and smells like perfume. The proverb constructs this primal contrast in one of its two terms, and this difference has the merit of lifting the taboo on masturbation. In no uncertain terms, the proverb erases religious taboos, in particular, sodomy (condemned by the Qur'an), which is invoked here in a truly epic space. Friendly sodomy? Language functions with automatic allusions, whose sociological feudal-patriarchal basis we can make out in passing: the Black servant and the prostitute are the privileged places of licit fornication (what is obscured here by this debauchery is related to the white married woman). A mysterious proverb (42) poses a delicate riddle: thanks to semantic loosening, the Black servant woman's ass turns black like henna on the hand (the meaning of the word *ndam* comes from a truly rare connotation surrounding black henna). There's a jubilant image substitution behind the scenes, where we can see a matchmaker holding a rosary. What could be more sacrilegious?

Minor Argument

If I claim false knowledge, who would listen to me? Knowledge that wouldn't transgress the taboo word (how could it?). Rather, a light, diaphanous, hilarious transvestism.

I would like it so much if this discourse was made up only of bagatelles: tautologies; clichés; stereotypes; canned phrases; ritual locutions; smooth, flat, felted phrases, crazy and humble at once. So many preparations for a spoken word that never fully reveals itself. It's through hilarious laughter that we can trick knowledge, making it so vulnerable to systems that we'd kill it simply by breathing words into it, by breathing through it.

But this false knowledge isn't an idealized speculation about laughter. It steps forward as a *strategic* reading of popular culture, repressed by logography. It seems to me that in this relation to oral literature, an intensified theatricalization directly bestows a more exact practice to the concept of writing.

Annex I

Transcription System

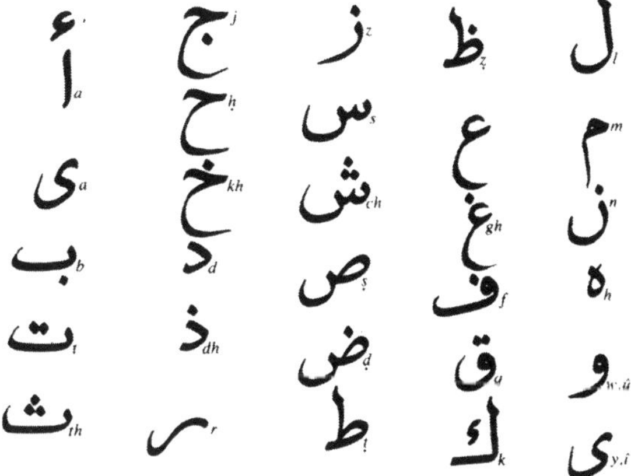

Figure 1.3. Arabic Transcription System.

Annex II

Corpus: Arabic Proverbs

1. illa hzal kûl ar-râs oula sman kûl ar-râs
2. dhan râsû b-la'sal ou dḥâh f-ghâr nḥal
3. ar-râs bla nachwâ qt'i'û ḥlâl
4. sâ'at zhû ma-ndûzha wa-law b-qti' ar-râs
5. illi maktûb fî jamjama ma yamḥîh ma
6. laqra' biflûsû ara dâk ar-râs nbûsû
7. ghîr tfût ar-râs ou tjî fîn ma bghat
8. 'illa 'âch ar-râs ma' adamtû châchiya
9. b-râs laḥmaq kaytqâ' al-wâd
10. bḥâl ch'ar fi-l'jîna
11. ch'and al-qar'a ma tar'â ghîr al-macht'a ou khyût' rashâ
12. 'aynak mîzânak
13. illî t'ârt 'aynû ḥafra bqat
14. ta'lâ al'ayn ḥattâ ta'lâ ou jî al ḥâjab fûq mannha
15. tamchî yâm lakhdîdât ou tjî ayyâm lawlîdât
16. chwârab dâda f-lbarrada
17. llâh ynijjîk ma najjâ lsân man bayn snân
18. lsan yad'ḥak lsan wa lqalb fîh lakhdî 'a
19. al-foum al-masdûd ma tadukhlû dabbana
20. taya't'i llâh al-foul ghîr lima 'andou snân
21. qad fammou qad drâ'û
22. qaḥba wa bzaqhâ man 'andhâ
23. d'arbou l-ḥalqû yansâ lli khalqû
24. mankhrû fij-jîfâ wa houwa kayqûl yakh
25. illâ lḥaqti l-widinîk ghîr 'ad'hâ
26. bḥal oudinîn l-kayyal
27. t-fakrat jadda khrîq wadnîha
28. illâ chattî laḥyat khûk tḥasnat ghîr fazzag l-ḥîtak
29. igalla' man llaḥyâ ou dîr fich-chârab
30. iddû f-yad khâh
31. illi d'arbtû yaddû ma yabkî
32. yaddi ou yadd l-qablâ ou yakhrouj laḥrâmi 'war
33. yaddîn l-qawwada fi-tsâbîḥ
34. kâlt al-yad ma tcham snîn
35. illî masa' dû fî sdar mayakoul jnâḥ
36. l-masâran fi-lkarch kayaddabzou
37. 'châyâ f-karchi ou d'awi f-'ayniyya

38. masabchi karchou ichabba'ha ou 'assâk 'al-qahba yatba' ha
39. 'allamnahoum t-zoumîl sabqûna l-zbâb l-kbâr
40. illâ sabbaḥti 'la al-machqûq ghîr sir lassûq
41. t'abboun ach-chalḥa fîh al-malḥa
42. ya't'i ou ndam bḥâl sawwat lakhdam
43. brad man sawwat l-ḥawwat
44. zab l-ma'rifa kaywâssá l-karr
45. ḥatta ḥazqat' âd d'ammat rajliha
46. rajlîn litîm kayjibou l-ghîs fî smaym
47. kayadkhoul bîn dfar ou lḥam bḥal lûsakh
48. mayḥouk jaldak ghîr t'afrak

Annex III

Translations

French

1. S'il maigrit mange-lui la tête; s'il grossit mange-lui la tête.
2. Il enduit sa tête de miel et l'introduit dans la ruche.
3. Tête morose? La trancher est permis.
4. Je ne «rate» aucun moment de jouissance même si l'on me coupait la tête.
5. L'écrit dans le crâne ne s'efface point.
6. Teigneux argenté, donne la tête à baiser.
7. Dépassée la tête advienne que pourra.
8. Si la tête vit (encore) elle trouvera toujours chéchia.
9. Avec la tête de fou on atteint la rivière.
10. Comme les cheveux dans la pâte.
11. De quoi s'occupe une chauve sinon de son peigne et de ses cheveux.
12. Les yeux sont ta balance.
13. Tes yeux envolés, il reste deux trous.
14. Aussi haut que les yeux pourront s'élever, le cil est dessus
15. Les jours/petites joues passentviennent les jours/petits enfants.
16. Les lèvres de Dada dans l'amphore (remarque: *Dada* signifie *nègresse*).
17. Que Dieu te protège comme il protège la langue d'entre les dents.
18. La dent sourit à la dent et dans le cœur la traîtrise.
19. Bouche close, mouche n'y entre.
20. Dieu ne donne des fèves qu'aux édentés.
21. Son bras aussi large que sa bouche.

[Translator's note: This Annex contains Khatibi's French translations of the Arabic proverbs and my English translations of his French translations. This sort of "bridge" translation is not usually advisable, and I have decided to provide Khatibi's French translations so that readers can more clearly understand the process through which the English translations have been rendered. I have tried to stay as close to the French translation as possible, making sure to retain a body part in each proverb, since we know from the first chapter that these proverbs are remembered through the mnemonic device of being mapped onto the body.]

22. Une putain, et la salive vient d'elle.
23. Frappe-le à la gorge; il oubliera celui qui l'a créé.
24. Le nez dans la charogne et il dit: ikh.
25. Si tu atteins ton oreille, mords-la.
26. Comme les oreilles du vendeur de blé.
27. À quoi pense la grand-mère au trou de ses oreilles?
28. Si tu vois la barbe de ton frère rasée, mouille la tienne.
29. Ce qu'il prend de la barbe il le mêle aux moustaches.
30. La main dans la main de son frère.
31. Celui qui est frappé par sa main ne pleure pas.
32. Ma main et la main de la sage-femme, et le bâtard sort borgne.
33. Les mains de l'entremetteuse dans le chapelet.
34. La main qui a mangé est rassasiée pour longtemps.
35. Qui n'a point mangé la poitrine ne peut atteindre les ailes.
36. Les intestins dans l'estomac se disputent.
37. Mon dîner dans l'estomac, ma lumière dans les yeux.
38. Ventre creux ose suivre la putain.
39. Nous leur avons appris la pédérastie; ils nous ont dépassés par la taille de leur verge.
40. Si tu as commencé ta journée en baisant une femme, tu peux alors aller au souk.
41. Le vagin de la Chleuh est salé (remarque: Chleuh: Berbère du Sud marocain).
42. Il donne et se repent comme le cul des servantes.
43. Plus froid que le cul du pêcheur.
44. La verge qu'on connaît élargit le cul.
45. C'est après avoir pété qu'elle joint les pieds.
46. Les pieds d'orphelin apportent la boue estivale.
47. Ne glisse entre chair et ongles que la saleté.
48. Rien ne frotte mieux ta peau que tes propres ongles.

English

1. If it's skinny, eat the head; if it's fat, still eat the head.
2. He coats his head with honey and puts it in the hive.
3. Headache? Cutting it off is halal.
4. I don't "miss out" on any possible joy, even if they cut off my head for it.
5. What's seared into the mind can never be erased.
6. O rich bald man, let me kiss your pasty pate.
7. Just spare the head; anywhere else is fine.
8. If the head is (still) alive, it will no doubt find a chechia.
9. With a head full of brimstone, we conquer the river.

10. Like hairs in pasta.
11. What would a bald woman worry about if not her comb and her hair?
12. Your eyes weigh things out.
13. With your eyes stolen, you're left with two holes.
14. However high your eyes might rise, they're still beneath your eyelashes.
15. The days/having little cheeks that comeandgo the days/having kids.
16. The Negro woman's lips on the amphora.
17. May God protect you like he protects your tongue between your teeth.
18. One tooth smiles to another while betraying it in its heart.
19. Close your mouth if you don't want a fly to fly in.
20. God doesn't give fava beans to the toothless.
21. His arm is as big as his mouth.
22. A whore, and from her we get saliva.
23. Hit him in the throat, and he'll forget who created him.
24. Sniffing the corpse, the nose says, "Yuk."
25. If you can, bite your ear.
26. Like the ears of a wheat seller.
27. What does the grandma think in the hole of her ears?
28. If you see your brother's beard shaven off, wet yours.
29. What he takes from his beard he rubs into his moustache.
30. The hand in the hand of her brother.
31. The person struck by his own hand never cries.
32. My hand and the hand of the midwife, and the bastard is born half blind.
33. The matchmaker's hands fingering the rosary.
34. The hand that has eaten is full for days.
35. He who has never tasted the breast has no chance to taste the wings.
36. Guts in the stomach argue.
37. My dinner in my stomach, a light in my eyes.
38. A hollow belly dares follow the whore.
39. We taught them pederasty, then they showed us what big dicks could do.
40. If you start your day by fucking a woman, then you're okay to go to the market.
41. The Shilha's pussy is salty.
42. He puts out then feels guilty like the servant girls' asses.
43. Colder than the fisherman's butt.
44. The dick that we know makes the asshole smile.
45. It's only after farting that she puts her legs together again.

46. The orphan's feet bring summer mud.
47. Only saltiness slips between flesh and fingernails.
48. Nothing better than your own fingernails to scratch your itch.

Chapter 2

Tattoos

Writing in Dots

A Dot, a Nib

What attracts our attention is the migration of one sign (or symbol) to another, however minute (a dot for example), and, little by little, the widening displacement of graphemes—this extraordinary repertory of objects extending, for example, from a cave painting to calligraphy, or to a rug, a tattoo, a basket, or an embroidered scarf. Yet, this tremor of signs is nothing other than the productive motif (itself itinerant) of our interrogation: the displacement of signs in a wandering series whose graphic representation sometimes vibrates in an efflorescence of meaning and sometimes freezes this migration in place, effectively erasing the gyratory space until it is reduced to a dot, a nib.

Where should we start? When Albrecht Dürer was asked to recreate a scene from the book of Revelation, he drew an angel with spread wings pointing a stylus at the forehead of a genuflecting priest. Perhaps we will never be able to know if the angel's stylus was a *qalam* or a nib used for tattooing, but never mind! An archaeology of knowledge will allow me to question and lay claim to this suspended gesture: history will teach me if such tattooing was possible. The enigma will be erased by historical discourse: in one case (tattooing), as in the other (writing on the forehead of the priest), the nib will have a place. Each will ask me to imagine the result of a similar substitution. In doing so, the entire destiny of the gesture will be changed for the angel–tattoo artist and the angel-engraver. Reflections of this gyratory movement in the mirror will separate and then fall into the historical record of meaning. But it is a hasty substitution. For what will history tell me, if not how history will project into me through a naive fraud (here, it is mnemonics that keeps meaning alive) the fantastical terrain of a mad identity?

Of course, I will have to articulate the life of the intersemiotic trace. For example, I will search in cave paintings for the analogous form that still exists in paintings or in tattoos or in tapestries. Or I will search with great care for an archaic dance step in a rug's motif. Confining myself within this dazzling, circular identity, I will be able to breathe. To write the intimate correspondence of the dispersal of signs, I will have to compose and recompose my body according to a technique of relaxation and wisdom, which will lead me finally to the belief that death *writes* for me, in my place, the increasingly stark outline of my solitude: a dot, a nib. And nothing will prevent me from thinking that masked death (of which archaeology is a slightly crazy rebus) prepared a celebration, or rather the image of a celebration, for my own pleasure. To efface my disorder in a fable-like sign, a glance cast at an animal engraving will suffice.

1. The Double Prohibition

This pleasure, as desirable as it is, must declare its theoretical basis. Let us agree for the moment that writing (in its broadest sense) includes all semiotic systems, both visual and spatial, and that the classic distinction between pictograph and logograph proves to be largely illusory. Jacques Derrida proved how Western knowledge (since the Greeks) is tied to the question of writing. The fundamental categories (intelligible/sensible, presence/absence, etc.) go back to an ideological system by which the West fastened its history (its *épistémè*) to a logographic adventure, effectively repressing all graphic writing that cannot be contained within the horizon of its metaphysics. Speech is primary, and language is the expression of speech (having content that transcends speech). The written mark simply camouflages this movement: the written mark is the double disguise of content that is forever elsewhere. Derrida denounces the logocentric vagaries still present in the fields of linguistics and semiotics—sciences that we now consider to be the most rigorous of the social sciences. Reconsidering the sign and the concept of the sign along these lines leads to the breakdown of our belief in metaphysics. Derrida's inscribed sign (the trace) is a sign without origin, a sign lodged inside the most violent difference.[1] This is from where the tattooed person and tattooed writing arise. Let us say that this deconstruction of Western knowledge responds to our desire: the subordination of our culture to the West calls for a similar decentering. The Derridean gesture permits the reconsideration of the status of less logocentric cultures:[2] Chinese culture or Arab culture has already thought out the concept of the sign in other terms. The best-known (though still poorly understood) example is that of calligraphy, which, in a manner of speaking, integrates the two faces of the sign—the signifier and the signified—within its combustive textual production. In calligraphy's movement, the inscribed trace creates knowledge in the largest form of materiality: a dot, a nib, a sign not exactly without origin but rather a sign whose very movement is the gyratory space of our interrogation, of our erasure.

It will be necessary to provisionally allow this reversal of values, which ties speech to the written mark, in order to accept—as we do—that tattooing is "writing in dots" (the phrase Arabs sometimes use for it), that it falls under the rules of a form of knowledge, a savoir faire, a desire, the circulation of signs sometimes inscribed on the body and sometimes migrating to other spaces, signs whose original symbol has often been lost to us but whose still-living inscription defies our theories of the sign.

The orthodox linguist will tell us that tattooing is indeed a semiotic system but very secondary, very marginal; that it is not even a language because it does not abide by the economy of double articulation. The linguist will then tell us something like this: *Before approaching your object (tattoos), please begin by constituting a new discipline, graphematics, which will allow you to analyze the combinatorics specific to each semiotic system. We will then see whether it will be possible—and I doubt it will be—to construct a general comparative theory. Intersemiotics does not exist.*[3]

Yet this method does not articulate the metaphysical presuppositions that define it. Operating on the assumption that the purpose of science is to accumulate facts and refine methods, we delegitimize the very question of the graphic sign, that is to say in no uncertain terms, the creative life of the sign. But we know, since Lacan, that the "tip of desire" does not follow the same path: the inscribed sign is not a simple veil, a disguise; it has a strategic position in the discourse of the unconscious.

This response of orthodox linguists—which is reductive, repressive, and obsessed with accumulating knowledge (but what exactly is being accumulated?)—is anathema to the approach that opposes it, which considers the written mark to be not the pretext of transcendental knowledge but the domain of an astonishing variety of writing systems whose radically divergent and unique trajectories must be acknowledged.

There is another reason why we are interested in tattoos: their ban by the principal monotheistic religions, as though divine writing wanted to hide all other forms of writing, especially the written mark on the body, behind its palimpsest. While biblical texts are fundamentally ambiguous (the symbol and the parable dominate their discourse), we can now suggest that religion, by being linked to logography, has pushed tattoos into the field of the profane and impure. It is for this reason alone that it is necessary to return to the repressed forms of arche-writing that abide in us.

We wonder if the sign of Cain in Genesis and the mark of God in the book of Revelation were tattooed signs.[4] In Genesis, it is said, "But the Lord said to them, 'Anyone who kills Cain will suffer vengeance seven times over.' Then the Lord put a mark on Cain."[5] It seems the mark was placed on his forehead. According to James George Frazer, the mark that God left on Cain's forehead as a sign of reprobation would not have clearly indicated that he was Abel's murderer.[6] Instead of being a signal, a hint, it would have been a symbol stronger than death. Whatever history's explanation, the bodily mark inscribed between brothers, between brothers and their father (God), is the place where the logographic inscription and the divine myth of the original trace are linked. God lays claim to the mark by giving it an origin.[7] And any origin myth is metaphysically like Borgesian rhetoric, which after being proliferated in cyclical time while searching for the word—the one word that could bring back the world—becomes immobilized, stuck in the very gesture that set it in motion and that brought it into being.

Other biblical passages mention a branding mark, a sign of humiliation and servitude; the Western world would later implement this system for the registration of prisoners and deportees. In Exodus, Moses says, "This observance will be for you like a sign on your hand and a reminder on your forehead that this law of the Lord is to be on your lips."[8] And in the book of Revelation:

> Then I saw another angel coming up from the east, having the seal of the living God. He called out in a loud voice to the four angels who had been given power to harm the land and the sea: "Do not harm the land or the sea or the trees until we put a seal on the foreheads of the servants of our God." Then I heard the number of those who were sealed: from the tribe of Judah 12,000 were sealed. And 12,000 from the eleven other tribes [of Israel].[9]

And this verse: "On his robe and on his thigh he has this name written: King of kings and Lord of lords."[10] And also this: "You shall not make for yourself an image of anything in heaven above or on the earth beneath or in the waters below."[11]

In the Bible, this type of mark is used to illustrate the sign of faith, which is to say, to distinguish the faithful from others. It's a system of classification separating believers and others, free men and slaves, women and prostitutes; in short, we find again the binary division of purity and impurity. Later, cultures influenced by Judeo-Christian thought will reject tattooing, placing it in the domain of the wild, the despicable, and the mentally ill. The observations of the criminologist Lombroso are quite comical:

> Nothing is more natural than to see a usage so widespread among savages and prehistoric peoples reappear in classes which, as the deep-sea bottoms retain the same temperature, have preserved the customs and superstitions, even the hymns, of the primitive peoples, and who have, like them, violent passions, a blunted sensibility, a puerile vanity, long-standing habits of inaction, and very often nudity.[12]

Obviously, we no longer make such preposterous claims, and on the Côte d'Azur after World War II we could admire women in bathing suits whose bodies were decorated with temporary tattoos that reproduced in lavish detail the paintings of the most famous modern painters. These women had to be aware of the upset caused by this written garment that is the tattoo. But this fad couldn't last, because it was against the economic principles of fashion. Returning to tattoos would have provoked a fearsome competition with clothing.

What does this have to do with Islam? The Qur'an is silent on the subject of tattoos, but one hadith clearly says, "The Prophet (PBUH) cursed the women who practice tattooing and those who seek to be tattooed."[13] Tattooing becomes as serious as usury. When writing in dots replaces sacred writing, the sacred hierarchy of signs—a logographic hierarchy, established by a divine decision and a transcendental discourse—risks being destroyed. In the circulation of systems and discourses, the profane reading of the body clearly must obey a doxological code, the only one capable of veiling the ecstatic letter and the chaotic body. But Islamic mysticism (in its most provocative form) will play with the two codes, will neutralize them through a subversion so strong that we no longer know which code is obscured in all this. We are referring to that *bismillah* tattooed on the pubis of the courtesans of Benghazi.[14]

We will also recall these lines of the pre-Islamic poet: "I remember Fatima's face, / Which, when tattooed / And veiled, became so sweet."[15] Nevertheless, the religious condemnation of representational art remains ambivalent: we can ask ourselves if this prohibition (against pre-Islamic idolatry) did not paradoxically reinforce the forms of writing that religion wanted to suppress; we will see later how calligraphy admirably transgressed this prohibition while staying faithful to the divine word. That is why the debate over figuration is a secondary concern here: it's the West that gives it undue attention.[16] Not only was (fundamentally abstract) representation capable of coexisting with the figurative arts (in particular, with miniatures, which are contemporaneous in the Arab world with shadow-puppet theater), but it has become, despite the more or less explicit prohibition, a generalized repertory of signs.

This double prohibition—religious and theoretical—justifies our interest in tattoos and speaks to another aspect of our current history: the elites of countries still under Western domination defend the idea of a national culture, or a positivism that is nothing other than the ideological mark of the petite bourgeoisie. In the name of national culture, we censure, we repress the values of popular culture, which are less logographic and more sensitive to a historical continuity of bodies. It is through the criticism of this ideology that knowledge can be built in theory and can play out in an art of living.

2. Stigma, *Wachma*, Tattoos, Writing

Stigma (Greek noun; *stigmatos*, genitive): the mark of a hot iron or a pointed instrument; tattooing in keeping with religious practices and other tattooing, according to Herodotus.[17]

Stizo (verb): to prick, to mark with a hot iron or a pointed instrument, to brand a horse, to punctuate. Three types of inscriptions are mentioned here: social markings of class (to identify an animal, a person, a slave); tattoos; and punctuation, which bears witness to the impossibility of removing the pictographic system (punctuation) from a linguistic space. It is necessary to reconsider how punctuation functions in discourse. The word *stigmate* (seldom used in French) and the archaic word *matacher* disappear in favor of *trace*, *mark*, *inscription*, and of course, *writing*. Do not forget the tip of desire in Lacanian rhetoric. The frequency of the word *pointe* ("nib") is astonishing in Michel Foucault.

Wachma (*wachama*, verb). The encyclopedic dictionary *Lisān al-ʿarab* gives the following remarks:[18] *wachma* indicates the tattoo that a woman makes on her arms (and that is called the "lines of the gazelle") with a needle coated with burnt fat. The tattoo can also be temporary, done with henna.

We say "Wachmat al-ardʾ" (The earth tattoos itself) when a bit of grass grows. Likewise, for the sky, when lightning flashes. Or by analogy, for a girl, when her breasts begin to grow. When I say that there is *wachm* between you and me, I mean that there is a conflict between us: the trace of evil demands that desire move like a palimpsest. *Wachama* is close to the root of *wasama* (to brand), which leads to the supposition that there is a close connection between human tattooing and the propitiatory sacrifice of a newly born animal taken from the herd (the ritual marking of animals) during the pilgrimage to Mecca.[19]

This metaphorical chain generalizes writing to an anthropomorphic level while occluding meaning in a circular symbol; this effectively translates the tension that exists at the heart of Islam between pre-Islamic writing and the rhapsodic writing-cum-fiat of the Qurʾan, conceived as an irreversible surpassing of all later forms of writing. The word *wachma* continues to be used in Arabic literature.[20]

The Polynesian word *tattoo* comes from *tatau* or *tatahou* (*ta*, "to draw"). James Cook wrote it down for the first time as *tattow* (which has become the English verb *tattoo*). It is a word infrequently used in French outside of its literal meaning. The author of these pages has not forgotten that the circulation of this word in one of his texts is troubling for those who know of tattoos only as marks of humiliation (on the bodies of prisoners or deportees).[21]

We will multiply the connotative play in the lexical ambiguity of/among these three words *stigma*, *wachma*, and *tatahou*—their simple musicality, the sparkling echo of their drama. Here, to write means to suspend cultural narcissism; to avoid learned transposition in order to achieve a productive disinterestedness; and to thereby locate, and lose track of, the meaning of all scriptural forms—without (school's) theoretical or methodological ruse—in the evanescent trace of several root words.

3. The Geometric Game

The limitations of writing—one major form of our imagination—are by now clear: the audiovisual seems to inaugurate the technosymbolic decline of the hand. Perhaps it will change the cycle linked to the relation between the spoken and the written. It seems to us that the semiotic is born in the loss of such an economy of the body.

Mallarmé already analyzed this fissure as it pertains to the basic community of forms noted by André Leroi-Gourhan:[22] technique, language, and figuration. Mallarmé's variations on the pure sign engender a chaotic retranslation, a space forever rewritten whose center and figures, while dispersing in a game of chance, are defined by an inscription liberated from literary representation.

The following movement provides one fugitive glimpse into this intersemiotic poetics:

> *The dancer is not a woman dancing*, for these juxtaposed reasons: that *she is not a woman*, but a metaphor summing up one of the elementary aspects of our form: knife, goblet, flower, etc., and that *she is not dancing*, but suggesting, through the miracle of bends and leaps, a kind of corporal writing, what it would take pages of prose, dialogue, and description to express, if it were transcribed: a poem independent of any scribal apparatus.[23]

The "dancing person" is a theoretical limit of language, or, more precisely, the dancing person lives in the suspension between the spoken word and the written word: the dancing person writes the spoken word and destroys it; the dancing person pulls from space a rigorous and polyphonic geometry—a whirlwind of codes, a mirage of written marks, an erasure of the trace by which the origin announces and consumes itself.

It is not about returning to a "natural" origin and to the illusion of nature's open book, like writing on sand or prints in snow, through which the hunters of the Upper Paleolithic and Mesolithic times communicated. The return to the pictography of the snow carpet leads us straight to totemism.[24] Our text tries to demonstrate the materialism of the hand's movement and the written mark. At the outset of human culture, writing was linked to the materiality of the hand's movement and the written mark, and all its history has consisted in reducing their pluridimensionality and polyphony in order to conceive of them through linearity.[25] Calligraphy only widened the gap between the spoken and the written; it will be considered, at best, a trope. But we will see that calligraphy is an intoxicating rhetoric, which explodes the linguistic sign. Its process rejoins the intersemiotic suspension of Mallarmé: the calligraphic stroke buries the linguistic sign in geometry and disperses it in the Platonic artifice of forms. The calligraphic letter is no longer exactly a letter but rather something between a letter and a musical note.

Let us go back to the case of tattooing. Let us begin with Février's contention that "it is with the material sign, the heir of the symbol, that writing truly begins."[26] Writing was a unique composition, a reduction of the hand's movement and the written mark. Meanwhile, thanks to gestural figuration, humans were able to move signs from one space to another. So, a tattoo is written on the body in a characteristic inflection of the hand and of the ideographic and pictographic trace.[27] A tattoo exists in the gap between sound and the written mark, a gap that defines what we normally mean by writing. Tattooing arises in this instability of semiotic systems. In its own way, it deploys pictographic movement. As a witness to an archaic form of writing, tattooing acts, almost unchangingly, in the domain of a difference so forgotten and so foreshortened that the scene opens upon a decorative meditation on death. I bring together these two words (*decoration* and *death*) intentionally: we think that the avoidance of meaning and interpretation is the worst violence that we can inflict on knowledge. To dispossess the body in this way, to betray the hierarchy of its values, and to affix, by whirling artifice, a false mask of death—it is through this rhythm alone that the tattoo is born, a decorated body whose scriptural nudity removes death. It is not a matter of magic, or of a theoretical sleight of hand in regard to writing, but it is theorizing the simple prolongation of a point of view with/against us, under whose angle the body-object no longer exists in the tattooed body. Thus, to weaken one type of knowledge about writing, to transform it into decoration, is to proceed unstably to the extreme end of productive disinterestedness.

In its essence, the tattoo is an ideopictographic motif. What is fascinating is that humans never stop giving themselves over to the geometric vibration of dead signs: the motif of a tattoo, of a carpet, of pottery, of a patterned scarf. The connections among these systems are far from being clear, but the connection between tattoos and pictography is now known. Février writes:

> In this particular case, we understand even more clearly, however in a much more evolved form, the relation between tattooing and written signs. We allude to the mysterious writing of Nsibidi. It was practiced at the start of the century by the members of a secret society in southern Nigeria. It isn't even clear that it was a system of writing in the strict sense, which is to say, a system for the notation of speech in its full form. It is rather a collection of symbols, of ideograms, each of which has a magical value unto itself. They are often tattooed on the body. They generally have a heightened pictographic character, and the origin of their meaning can be established in many cases: if the meaning often escapes someone who isn't initiated, it is more than clear to someone to whom the more or less schematic system of representation has been explained. And so the sign for money corresponds to bent leather bars; the sign for the conflict of contradictory acts of testimony is two lines, one straight and the other curvy, entangled in each other; the sign for the idea of commerce is symbolized by a man (a merchant) at the fork in a road. They are small, amusing enigmas more than they are a coherent system of writing. They remain interesting primarily, we repeat, for the relation they establish between the graphic sign and tattoos.[28]

But what can we hope to gain from a code whose contextual logic escapes us? The analyst following in Février's path would strive to their utmost to explain tattoos by the totemic mark, the differential mark that has relevance only in its position with respect to the metaphoric mode of classification.[29] This inevitable encounter with the spoken word led us to separate the analysis of geometric forms from onomastic reference. The game, thus defined, is the motif of the gyratory difference of which we willingly speak.

So, to summarize, tattooing, seen as a graphic game, runs up against a certain metaphysics of being. The loss of context leads to the loss of the original object, and geometric form leads to the disfiguration of the subject. A simple decorative motif plays a subtle role in the ruin of the dialectic of subject and object.

Methodologically, the graphic game has a very limited rhythm; it is confined to a small repertory of signs, several *stoicheïa*, which would permit—optimally—a mathematico-geometric construction. The repertory is not defined by a system of oppositions but involves the creation of a number of exercises from a dot, from a nib. The code that would be used is pure idiolect. Another methodological possibility would be to identify the "microphysical code" buried in our bodies.[30] But the obvious risk would be to return to the illusion of a biocosmogonic language inscribed in our body. It is true that acupuncture works like this, but the code of that other form of tattooing is discernible since it is used to cure sickness. For what would sickness be without a code?

Clearly, the stoicheïa trace their origins back to specific mythograms, some of which are still used, such as the hand in Arab culture. Their symbolic heft sometimes weighs on us, worries us. Subconsciously. But others, the majority, come into and out of life as hollow signs. Our future task will be to recompose them as a group through a timely reading suggested by a specific place in our text. It will still be necessary to allow a geometric pleasure to float in the critical space that pierces it.

To make this geometric wager—this loss of subject and object reabsorbed in the pure sign (and not in meaninglessness)—clear, we must revise the standard point of view on decoration (as part of tattooing or otherwise).[31] Different from the linear expansion of words, a system of graphic signs provokes a polyphonic game. Obviously, this is a rhythm lacking syntax, which belongs to language; it is a rhythm—a formula for meaning—in which everything is held obstinately inside the symmetrical circle, the horizon of myth, and unfolds in the pleasure of sophisticated candor. This is the only understanding of graphic representation that will allow us to write a tattooed woman. Or write to her, if you will. At the very least, this narrative perspective is suspended in a material gesture.

How could we write this woman? The creation of a body through our Moroccan corpus invokes a particular divine choice; the tattooed Muslim body obeys specific rules for implementation and spacing. For the most part, in Morocco we tattoo just one side of the body, the front, while Polynesians tattoo the entire body. Add to this one more difference: the woman can tattoo the front of her body, and the man can tattoo only his hand, arm, and forearm—that is to say that the hand never leaves the domain of writing. We tattoo the way we write, giving privilege to our right side, which does not destroy symmetry: lines are struck onto the body in a motif that is parallel to it and that passes over the forehead, over the chin, and between the breasts. Lines indicate desire. There is no center except the place of its own reading, of its own perversity, blessed by God or not.

Let us call this group of drawings decorating the body a "fabric": in the word *fabric*, there is the idea of a microphysical composition of material, the idea of a rhythmic space, and *last but not least*, the notion of writing. We will see that this play on words—like every art of the bagatelle—is valuable; in reality, certain motifs exist just as commonly on rugs as they do on tattooed bodies. Fabric does not obey any known syntax; it consists of a repertory of geometric figures that is easy to analyze. Let us call both fabric and the geometric forms that cross several semiotic systems "migratory signs." The goal is to dissolve our discourse through movement of this sort.

I asked how we can write this woman. I propose two exercises. The reader will have to choose one composition.

A) Basic Forms

These are the stoicheïa (see figure 2.1): the dot, or a series of dots (a tattoo can be as small as a dot, which was the basis of our introduction, if you recall); the straight line and the ornaments that come from it; cruciform ornaments; star ornaments; V-shaped ornaments; the chevron; the diamond; and the circle. The production of a piece of fabric is guided by two movements: a social idiolect, in which several signs suffice to produce a local semiotic system (a tribal semiotics, for example); and a personal idiolect, the style of the person making the tattoo. A repertory of signs such as this, which is often without meaning, does not seem to obey any rules prescribing its location on the body. It is the idiolect that decides.

B) The Subverted Body

Which graphic economy does the first body obey (see figure 2.2)? The choice of signs is aleatoric, in the sense that we remove them and draw them in correspondence with the fleeting moments of our pleasure—a pleasure made possible by a decision of disfiguration, namely, the subversion of the prohibitions that bind the Muslim body. This allows the expansion of other unnamed values and the implementation of signs with a different spatiality, annotated in a new manner on the different places of the body. By the spacing of pure signs, we are then able to generalize a rhythm for polyphonic reading.

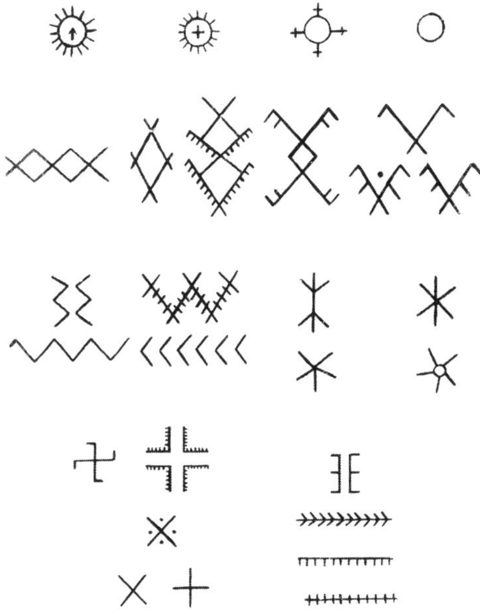

Figure 2.1. Tattoos: Basic Shapes.

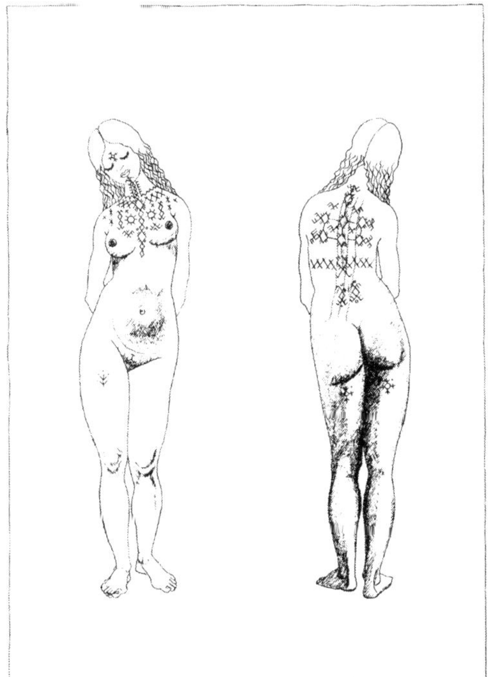

Figure 2.2. The Subverted Body.

We suggest that chance intervenes here, and that the center is a gyratory point that annihilates itself in the act of interpretation. This will be what helps us take back the body.

According to historians, boustrophedon (the turning of the ox) writing[32] was developed alongside agriculture. In such a system, "the visual economy of reading obeys a law that is analogous to that of agriculture."[33] Interpretation is suspended in a dual system of graphic representation that illustrates the relation between culture and nature: the human writes the way he works; eroticism develops from this movement. The Arabic word *khad'*, which means writing, calligraphy, and penmanship, also means a straight furrow, a dug-out line, or a line traced into sand by a finger or stick. Arabic calligraphy often invokes decorative motifs recalling this type of writing.

What does this have to do with our argument? A famous verse of the Qur'an says, "Your wives are [like] your fields, so go into your fields whichever way you like."[34] We could be justified in thinking, on the basis of this verse, that anal sex with a woman is acceptable—an interpretation contested by certain theologians. We will talk most directly of Islam, that boustrophedon place of our speech. But interpreting the metaphor in the sense of sodomy requires a hierarchy: fornication begins from the front, then precedes to the rear. If a man first penetrates the woman from behind, then, according to Jabir, misfortune will follow: the baby will be born with only one eye.[35] The order of sex follows a sacred rhythm. And sodomy, according to theology, is evil because the ass is the place of the devil. We would say it's all legend, but the sexual prohibitions analyzed by Freud invoke mythic discourse to no lesser degree.

The ideal Muslim rite adds the divine word—the enunciation of the first Qur'anic phrase, bismillah—to the pleasure of fornication. According to Cheikh Nafzawi, reading the Qur'an is good foreplay. The erotic is granted twice by God: by the Book and by the technical and ritual order by which each part of the body is accorded its function.

Let's return to the act as it announces and subverts itself, disfigures itself, on our decorated body. According to aesthetic paleontology, freeing the face and the hands from nature was a crucial separation. That the spatial symbolism of religion sets forth a repressive logic for the different bodily functions is not in the least surprising—the equilibrium that liberates the face (language) keeps the hand (figuration) within an ordered rule of values: the center (the trace of God) and the subject (a simulacrum of such an image) appear in overdetermined locations on the body.

Always linked to this metaphysical horizon, our *fore-play* consists of defining tattooed fabric in a general fashion. Fore-play: front, back. Displacement in this way: the back, the thighs, and the buttocks are now joined to our text. Fittingly, the scene of spatial concepts is reabsorbed in the time of desire. The permutation in the chain of semiotic terms, the creation of a pure sign (anaphora), by which it is necessary to take up again the cross-analysis of fabrics, inching outside the metaphysical circle. Acting as gestural transition in transition (this activity by which the scene is composed), tattooing is, with little theoretical overwriting, the undoubtedly banal state of a silence, a solitude.

In Islam, if the face is visible, it must be protected—either by the veil, of course,[36] or by its double, the tattoo; or by the double of the double, a tattoo in henna or in *ḥargûs*,[37] whose color intervenes to illustrate another migration. This leakage of repertory elements again marks the tension between logography and a system of graphic representation. The most important type of Moroccan tattooing is the *ʾayyacha* (between the eyebrows). The body is first split on the forehead, between the eyebrows. This often appears in a basic form: three vertical dots or three horizontal dots. Herber also writes of the use of a chevron, recalling a rug design, or even the ornamental circumference of cruciform motifs. Let us call this sign the "third eye" (*toë*). Traditionally, the toë protects against the evil eye,[38] but what is evil in our case? Here, the toë marks a double trajectory, in which the graphic economy of the precursor exchanges the sign (the eye) for another sign (the toë), the median organizing the body, one part against the other. Then, lower in the body, which has now been entered into a system of graphic representation, two doubles of the toë decorate the buttocks. The archaic triad finds a position that is symmetrically doubled, then annulled in the suspension of front and back: the fore-play of writing.

The *siyyâla* is a tattoo on the chin, drawn vertically from the lower lip to the bottom of the chin, then continued onto the throat and the chest with an ornament from a Berber rug. Herber asks naively, "Why don't the chest tattoos have any relation to the neckline of clothes?" Tattoos, as written clothes, defy voyeurism: the written clothes are a body. Their iconic fantasy is invoked in a simple and violent gesture of touching, and an orgasm travels through this in a choreographic mobility. The celebration of tattooing is anti-voyeuristic: its double game produces the pure sign originating from the body and vice versa, in the same way that the geometric game becomes indistinct (without a metaphysical fusion) and follows a gyratory movement—that is, a transgression that *travels*.

The *toë*, generalized fabric, and an ornament above the pubis (called *wachma fûgû*, literally "tattoo on top") carry over onto the back—this is our decisive motif—by three red lines: grafts, *qulams*. And so, with hardly any moral principles, the doxological body is occulted. This is the motif sketched out here, the movement of an artifice expanded in its milieu: the scriptural body. A red stripe.

C) The Woman-Number

Because of another artifice, the geometric universe gives way to another form of writing, this time based on a system thousands of years old and centered on the number five, or *khamsa*.[39] It is a pentagram usually known by the form of a starred polygon, but its creative possibilities are unlimited. The khamsa is a migratory sign that can be transformed into many geometric designs. From prehistory and the negative handprints of the Bovidian-era figures at Tassili to contemporary times and the hand of the Moroccan lottery, the pentagram stuns by its mobility: no subject can resist it. And yet, that is not to say that its decoration is simple: its schematics are extraordinarily varied (see figure 2.3). But taken as a *primary function*,[40] it creates a vertiginous interval between its inherent logographic symbolism and its annulment of the figuration-abstraction opposition. What interests us here is not the lexical richness of the pentagram (which is well known)[41] but rather its rhythm retranslating one semiotic system into another, its disconcerting capacity of *transport*. The pure sign doubles then departs; there is no rule of right-handedness. So, there is a third hand, just as there is a third eye. Usually a vertical motif or bar,[42] an open hand with an obvious prophylactic function (clear protection against the disorder of signs), the khamsa is a supreme signifier, by which the infinity of doubles is detheatricalized in this mobile, floating representation.

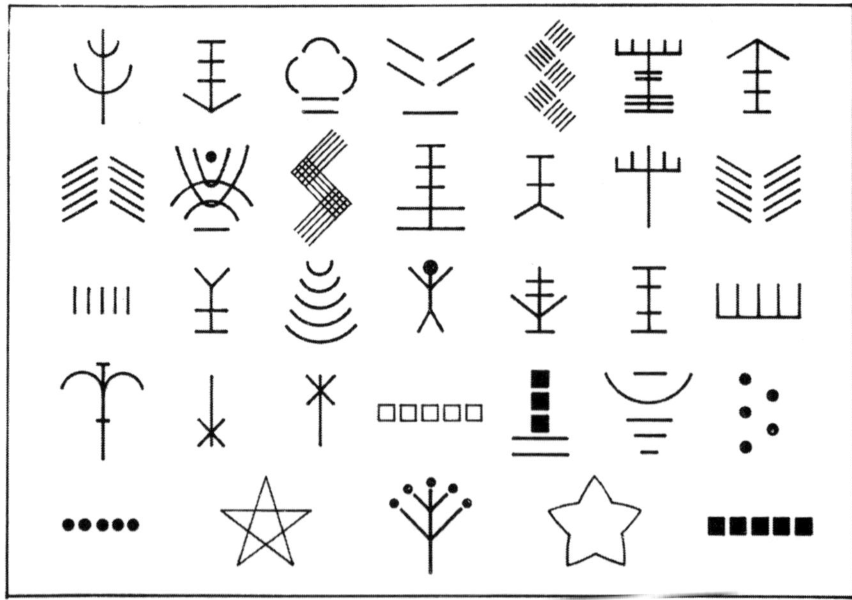

Figure 2.3. Pentagrams: Tattooed Forms of Five Elements.

There is no rule of right-handedness, which is replaced by the phallic iconography of the middle finger. When we say *khamsa 'la 'aynîk* (five on your eyes) or, more literally, *zob 'la 'aynîk* (penis on your eyes), we speak without doubt of a great desire—that of a letter intercalated inside a doubled gesture: the middle finger and the penis flip back and forth in the same insult, in the same hilarious laughter. This brings to mind the following childhood couplet:

khamsa 'la 'aynîk al-m'amchâ
tasbaḥ mt'amcha qad al-ḥamssa

five on your gummy eyes
to make them as hard as chickpeas

The middle finger of the child makes clear the contradictory body language of sexual repression. It is an exclusive, violent digit, animated by a drowned meaning: the paternal image is changed by outside laughter. But let us leave this anecdotal substitution of the middle finger of the right hand and return to another anecdote about pentagrams that has a more radical intersemiotic quality: in the Sahara, on the eve of a wedding, the *ḥannana* (woman who decorates hands with henna) removes the fiancée's henna, then touches the hand of the person nearest her, and so on until everyone in attendance is symbolically tattooed—a platonic gesture, an ultimate tattoo. This is a semiotic sleight of hand: the khamsa removes the tattoo, erasing that on which its existence is based and by which the virgin—before the breaking of the hymen[43]—gives herself over to a scattering of the sign and of space. We would also be tempted to dream diaphanously of another transport: the theoretical interval where pleasure and its rhythmic difference are erased.

But this slightly hysterical vision of female genitalia must be dismissed for the time being—for two reasons. The first is that this vision, according to popular tradition, can chase away a wild animal (or reader), and that is not our intersemiotic objective. The second is more divine: according to an interpretation that aligns with ours, the khamsa would be a material transposition of the name of God, God being the contraction of the article and the Arabic word for divinity.[44] But the hand far predates Islam, and so this explication is a moment of chaos quickly recuperated by the calligraphic game. We are still within the horizon of theology.

Having commented on these anecdotes, we can quickly locate the geometric game of the khamsa. In addition to having features that define it as an anaphora, the khamsa doubles its being as a number: the five becomes four or three (an archaic triad?), or simply *one* floating yet perceptible form. Each time, the doubled image erases the number that it represents. "I would like to die," says the number five. "Start by moving into the gap," respond the other numbers. Here, the gap makes concrete the rubric for a tattoo that we present as the "second immobile body" (see figure 2.4). It is a pendant made of five cowries strung horizontally, two above and three below.

Tattoos in numbers:
khamsa/vulva/rhythm.

Figure 2.4. Stitched Cowries.

4. An Economy of Signs

As written clothing, tattoos possess an elemental repertory of signs that resists theories of representation. We have spoken of the *geometric* image until now not because it is the origin of all tattooed ornaments but because this economy of the sign makes the act of interpretation pivot and adjust each time. So, our preceding fore-play subverts the doxological body by playing with the opposites of right/left and front/back and by suggesting another motif of symmetry.

In fact, these displacements do not remove us from the hold of doxology. It is necessary to take up the meditation on another level, in particular, that of the economy of exchange (of signs). An astonishing parallel exists between the system (economy) of tattooing and card games, a parallel admirably analyzed by Claude Lévi-Strauss.[45] What do we exchange while playing cards? There is a "graphic exchange": one illustrated sign replaces another in a repetition that dissolves the present, which, in relation to *truco*, suggested to Borges that "time is only a fiction."[46] The pleasure of playing is that of dissolution, the rupture of time, and a lax economy of the sign: we exchange one dead sign for another, a movement whose metaphysical importance we understand in the rhetoric of Borges. The Borgesian text is a perpetual erasure, an illusory apparatus of texts operating one against the other. Perhaps the final trick of Borges is to have transformed his immense erudition (his mobile library) into a false economy of exchange: the setting of myths and narratives and their rotating entanglement return ceaselessly to the figure of cyclical time. Borges is, without doubt, an innocent metaphysician who believes he is replacing one of our cards with another (one of our codes with another): this is how the cyclical game and Borgesian rhetoric hypnotize us within a symmetrical horizon.

The second exchange of the card game is a "strategy of desire":[47] the circulation of graphic signs that, in dissolving the present, is doubled by a silent discourse whose violence is an erotic and automatic writing (albeit regulated by an activated, *transitory* code), which suspends the gesture of the appropriation of the other. In a waking dream, the card player moves on an oblique axis where the symmetry of the written mark and of desire is ceaselessly foiled by a paradigmatic trembling. Look at a hand that plays cards: it throws cards obliquely.

The variety of tattooed fabric is dependent on the same oblique gesture. Symmetry is established through divine order, but the inscription on the body traces back to an archaic writing system from before the advent of divine symmetry. Tattooing allows this erotic duel between symmetry and asymmetry, this economy rife with a romantic expenditure and a doubled, theatrical desire. The tattooed body is a graphic mark that disfigures the notion of appropriation. It is a form of writing that demands to be read, loved, and desired in its exceedingly emotional, chaotic movement.

In accordance with popular culture, a young Moroccan woman can tattoo herself on two occasions: at puberty and at marriage. The bodily inscription supplements the economy of nature, as the written mark identifies the cycle of blood in the first case and the loss of the hymen in the second. Puberty is a disorder of somatic signs. To ritualize the erotic consists of redoubling suffering by the needle's tip. The fear of the pubescent girl is that of being swept away by a flood of blood; the tattoo is, then, a fiction of this fantasy, of this somatic disorder. It suggests a musical note—something incisive, grafted onto the body—that demands to be heard in the loneliest desire, the most silent, the most resistant to articulation.

The same is true for the hymen. By which form of body language should it be named? In this case, it is not sufficient to say that the tattoo is the link between nature and culture;[48] the hymen is a

> protective screen, the jewel box of virginity, the vaginal partition, the fine, invisible veil which, in front of the hystera, stands *between* the inside and outside of a woman, and consequently between desire and fulfillment. It is neither desire nor pleasure but in between the two. Neither future nor present but between the two. It is the hymen that desire dreams of piercing, of bursting, in an act of violence that is (at the same time or somewhere between) love and murder. If either one *did* take place, there would be no hymen.[49]

I don't have the time here to analyze Derrida's rigorously delirious essay on the hymen, but, by applying his analysis to the tattoo, I would escape anthropological and sociological reduction (we refer to the theory of rites of passage, but it is precisely the *passage* that is a problem) and better understand the rhythm of tattooing in the economy of signs, its antilogographic function, and the irreducibility of its mark.

I've suggested a parallel between somatic economy and graphic economy. We must clarify their many effects, which develop first from color. Because color tattoos are often temporary, they are done in henna and ḥargûs.[50] Blood—the color of abduction, the color of the disorder of signs—is an excess of a Freudian drive. It's the divine, paternal color, which introduces a hierarchy of separation in the rainbow. The loss of the hymen is not murder. It suggests the palimpsest and the theater: sometimes the bloody sheet of the marriage bed is shown in public. At the same time, red is the naturalized color that sets in motion the rotation of the rainbow's colors. Celebration: song, dance, culinary ritual, the hysterical cries of the bearer of the bloody sheet—so many swirling gestures that on this occasion give the tattoo the value of an overdetermined inscription.[51]

There are different ways of preparing henna, each meant for a specific part of the body, especially the hands and the feet. We will return later to the technique's details; for the moment, it is enough to say that after the henna is applied and dries, its crust is removed. The red-yellow color changes according to the rhythm of the days and disappears after ten to fifteen days. As the color *between* abduction and legal appropriation, *between* the hymen and the satisfaction of pleasure, henna lasts until sex is no longer difficult and laborious. To cook up sex, as we will see, is a precise art, an aphrodisiacal medicine of the most sophisticated sort, in which perfume will be a musical, gyratory place: written mark, perfume, music—this relay (so Baudelairean) will return as the subject of our text on Cheikh Nafzawi.

In the somatic énoncé, henna intervenes to cover the disorder of signs. Applied to virgins, it cures certain fever symptoms; mixed with alum and rose water, it tells a woman if she has syphilis (the "French disease"),[52] protecting children from venereal diseases. To stop their period, women drink water suffused with crushed henna. Likewise, to administer beauty remedies or to win someone's heart. Witness this unsettling custom:

> The woman who wants to surpass all others in beauty must burn the linen that a negro and a negress have slept in after having made love. She mixes henna into its ashes and then dilutes them with a little water. A paste is formed that will make her face radiant. If the linen of negros is not available, she can use that of a prostitute. But in either case, the linen must be stolen for the result to be effective.[53]

What we vaguely refer to as magic is this transfiguration of the body by the theft of erotic signs (property is its currency). The same symbolism that is at stake in a game of cards defines the economy of this system: the discourse of desire is continuously at play, as we exchange the violence of desire doubled by desire. From here springs mortal violence: in these examples, the erotic quality of henna is based on a relation of the color to the potion (poison and aphrodisiac), the one determining the other in a veritable whirlwind of codes.

The tattoo attests to this scene of simulacra through a group of signs marked by what we can call "mystical vaccination." The cross is the most banal element. It is written onto the arms of pilgrims returning from Jerusalem. The foreheads of Moroccan Jewish babies are tattooed with crosses. This practice takes place as well in the Sahara. This act of tracing a cross on an object—to sacrifice it in a sense, by cutting it into four symbolic parts—is an ancient tradition. To enact it in front of someone is to annul that person's potential power over you. The tattooed cross on the forehead sets the *toë* against the evil eye. Like all mysticism, this practice is based on a medical theory; cautery (the hot iron),[54] the tip of a needle, all these "needles of death" effectively have a medical purpose. This is made explicit by a Muslim exegete:

> [Curative] tattoos don't separate the flesh from the outside world as ornamental tattoos do; they are like bandages, and just as the wounded person is authorized by religious statute to replace ablution by lustration (lustration is, in this case, practically reduced to a simulacrum), the person who is tattooed because of illness is authorized to replace every act of bathing by a simulacrum.[55]

This distinction between ornamental tattoos (the arbitrary) and curative tattoos (the necessary) reconciles religious ideology with medicine. But our exegete remains silent on the final status of the first type of tattooing; he defines it simply by opposition, which returns to condemn it silently if without provocation. This is, in fact, the opinion of the Shafiʿi school, which only tolerates tattooing in the case of necessity: illness or physical blight. Ideological displacement is subtly in evidence: curative tattooing as a supplement to nature is no more than a guilty simulacrum. Suffering caused by the touch of a hot needle is added to illness or ugliness to indicate, with this *extra*, the permanent mark of God, of his presence. To accept a positive simulacrum made for the pleasure of the body would be a way of veiling the divine trace with erotic writing. It replaces God's order by a human strategy of desire.

Mystical vaccination participates in the general economy of signs. As a sign marking identity, a tattoo is linked to the circulation of objects and their appropriation. The signature imposed on the body migrates in the erotic game and the exchange of currency and plays out in the master-slave dialectic and the hierarchy of social groups. And, generally, tattooing is a heraldic principle, a fetishism charged with a masked animality and the death drive. What's a tribe? The (segmentary) tribal system obeys an institutionalized competition: me against my brothers; my brothers and me against my cousins; my brothers, my cousins, and me against the entire tribe; and the tribe against the whole world. In a system like this, which resembles a game of chess, tattoos participate in their own way in an economy of conflict. To be sure, we exchange women like we exchange words and economic goods, but in this circularity the tattoo doubles and redoubles exchange and introduces into the strategy of desire a basic geometric graphism, whose meaning is first lost and then simulated, forcing us to be attentive to the universality of these motifs (rugs, pottery, calligraphy, etc.) so as not to fall into nonsense and vertigo.

Its appropriation is multiple: as a simple safe-conduct or a talismanic passport (in a mnemonic process), the tattoo was the master's mark on a slave in Africa. Slaves were tattooed just as livestock were. It's also the fleur-de-lis of convicts under the French monarchy, or the symbol of certain sections of the Moroccan army in the precolonial period. Don't forget as well the brute symbols of those deported to Auschwitz: an ID number to which was added a letter corresponding to the transfer date and an uppercase delta, all tattooed on the left forearm with a stylograph.

These chaotic images interrupt the dance of the Polynesian coral fishermen whose nude, tattooed bodies scare off dangerous fish, and they bring us back to a fallen sovereignty: the tattoos of prostitutes. However, in the eroticism of this relation, simulation is suppressed by currency; in this elimination, the prostitute's tattoos will attain a nostalgia of the simulacrum, a comic scene, in which tawdry pearls, clownish shows, and tattoos of flowers, plants, architecture, and other stereotypical symbols will explode in an aggressively gawdy scintillation: the heart cleaved by an arrow. This is for the pleasure of the string puller: the pimp. The excess of madcap libertinage sets off Joseph Herber's imagination. Stunned, he writes, "It's strange that the prostitute announces on her skin, which professionally belongs to everyone, that her heart is reserved for one person alone."[56] At the very least, it would be a deathly sob. Or an eruption of obscene laughter. Or a way of making our own hand masturbate: writing.

To write deceitfully by a louche wink on the pubic tattoo, which is found more commonly on prostitutes than on anyone else. Geometric in its form, wachma fûgû—a tattoo on the shaved pubis (the ornament effacing the pubic hair)—makes apparent the lost economy of the sperm. And, without a doubt, we can exchange an ejaculation of sperm for a sum of money, but the erotic game is deceitful and becomes a crass parody.

We can even read the semiological history of colonization directly from the Moroccan prostitute's tattoo: the geometric patterns now combine with nongeometric designs—that is, images of flowers, plants, and trees (cypresses, palms)—as well as iconic architecture (what hilarious nostalgia to see a marabout's shrine drawn on the body of a prostitute!). Writing is visible here: these awkward calligrams are the eternal signature of the name of the "eternal lover." This rhetorical debauchery is visible in one example:

> A prostitute originally from Casablanca: the tattoo located above the upper lip is European; it and the dot tattooed on the left eyelid were done by a BILA soldier.[57] This woman, born in a town where tattooing is rare, had on her right arm (in the middle, anterior-exterior face) a pansy that was very skillfully tattooed; on her forearm of the same side (anterior face), a rabbit on top and the name "Chicken" in the middle. On the left arm (anterior-exterior face, in the middle) was a woman's bust, outlined with a very low Louis XV bodice, anchored to her shoulders with straps; her hairstyle was in keeping with the times. Next to this image, there was a flower; above it, the name "Lucien Coquard." On the forearm of the same side (anterior face, in the middle) was a woman's naked torso.[58]

It's a décor of tawdry baubles accompanied by symbols sometimes more opaque than moving. On one Moroccan prostitute's body, a drawing of camels was found in keeping with the cave art of Libyan Berbers; on another's, a drawing of a fish, itself harkening back to the ancient oriflamme fish, the ichthus symbol. Fire shines forth through an exaggerated nostalgia with an allegorical touch: a dot, a nib, a gyration of signs rendered theatrical in degeneration.

5. Needle/Qalam/Color

There are many techniques for tattooing. The tip of a Barbary fig can be used, or a pine needle. Sometimes a knife. But the preferred Moroccan tool is the needle. Each tattooer has a tool bag, just as a healer has a set of cures. The

Figure 2.5. Tattooed Face.

tattooer's personal recipe combines a wide variety of aromatic plants, charcoal, and spices. The protocol is as follows:[59] First, trace the desired designs with charcoal. Second, heat up the lampblack according to the recipe. Third, apply the lampblack with a needle, to the extent that the person can tolerate the pain; the application takes around twenty days. Fourth, gradually wash with salt water and aromatic plants until the scar forms. (See figures 2.5 and 2.6.)

Ḥargûs (temporary color tattooing) plays out over a larger palette. Ḥargûs is made by selecting ingredients from the following list:

- Chinese ink
- gallnut
- soot
- burnt oleander
- wood ash

Figure 2.6. Tattooed Face.

- spices
- tar
- sap of burnt vine stock
- walnut tree leaves
- lampblack
- oil
- alum
- dried black walnut bark
- kohl
- incense

Ḥargûs (like a regular tattoo) is a heated liquid, lampblack. The fundamental difference is that one is applied to the body with a needle and the other is applied to the skin with a qalam or the tip of a twig.

This ephemeral tattoo lasts for a day or two: the duration of a festival, a rite, a rut. Makeup, perfume, tattoos whose game is an erotic syllabary being said, being dissolved by color. On the face, the white, bluc, green, and red of ḥargûs; on the cheeks, the white stain (composed of henna, cloves, and cinnamon); inside and outside the irises, the sultry gray of kohl. Henna, added to gallnut and cloves, turns black; added to garlic and sal ammoniac, it also turns black. And so the night falls ("Forgive me that evening hath come on," Zarathustra said[60]). And so, overcome by trembling lips, I sing and I dance (sec figure 2.7).

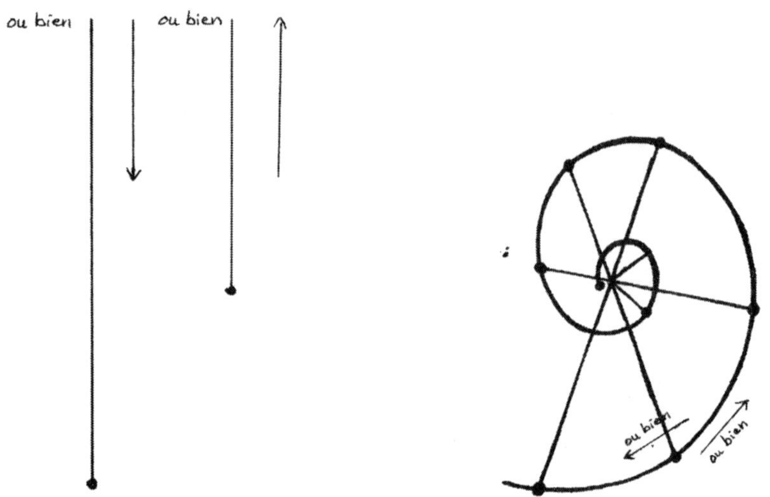

Figure 2.7. Spiral, after Paul Klee.

The water mill says to the hand mill, "Sleep, then.
When the water of the lock climbs, how many loads I'll mill!"
The hand mill replies. He says,
"I don't envy your solitude in the waters of gardens,
Because my house is graced with the tribe of sweethearts.
Tattooed hands make me turn."[61]

This is a mythic chant that imagines, because of a bout of madness, the usage of the homonymy of opposites (the *ad'd'ad* in Arabic), composed of a rotation of signs (except for number 1 below) around the absence of color (black):

1. *aḥmaru*: red/white
2. *akhdaru*: green/black
3. *aswadu*: black/white
4. *safrâ'u*: yellow/black

Denying the gesture of writing, the word *lamaqa* (or *namaqa*) means at once to write and to erase. It contains a mortal lyricism for the white page, began with the letter, then dispersed in color. The thing by which, again, gyratory movement leads us to one and one thing alone: the spiral. "There it's a question of life and death, and the decision depends on the little arrows," says Paul Klee.[62]

6. Naming (Onomastics)

There's no representative correspondence between the tattooed drawing and its naming procedure.[63] The name can be a simple tautology, and in this case the drawing carries the same name as the place on the body where it's found: for example, *sdar* (chest), *ûchâm allaḥya* (chin tattoo, or beard, in the word's literal sense). It's a split name that covers up a game at once flat and ambivalent: this is the rhetorical game most resistant to analysis. And the most treacherous. Who ties down the other? The drawing or the body?

Close to a tautological procedure, the name of the image marks the signature: *t'aba'* (tattoo between the eyebrows: stamp, seal), *tasnîda d-Lalla Fatima Zahra* (chin tattoo: consecration to Lalla Zahra, the daughter of the Prophet). Likewise, *khatam slimaniya*, the seal of Solomon drawn on the wrist or the hand. Both ornamentation and talisman, a tattoo there protects against the evil eye, or so it's said. The saintly or prophetic signature is, however, doubled: a genealogical image, it traces back to the sacred text and the origins of the discourse of desire; at the same time, deduction (although naturalized, cinched closed, and given as divine) contorts in a sign indicating the movement by which it will achieve the other. In a discourse of protection and security, there's always an erotic illusion. Belonging to God, the body is this nudity without exchange between the heavens and the earth: God provides; humans transcribe. But the inscription of the tattoo disfigures the illusion of sacred property: the ornamentation frees itself from any semiotic system; in turn, it inscribes another text, another body, and creates a false dispossession of nudity. It seems to me that this is a valid assertion for all whirlwinds of signs marked by the illusion of belonging to a divine taxonomy, given as well that the fear of the evil eye maintains the disorder of the sign in its fullest form.

A third category speaks of the gestural image: *t'allâla* (that which looks; between the eyebrows) or *'awâmma* (that which swims; on the shoulders). These are images closer to calligraphy (a calligraphy without language) than to pictography in its strictest sense because no spatial relation exists between the sign and its referent. The gestural image is an erotic transport: in t'allâla, it's a third eye that marks the game. There is a displacement of seeing: what reads me, what makes me see, isn't a natural vision but something between natural vision and its substitute. There is already a theater of frisson and uncanny confusion. Naming a geometric sign to supplement vision can only bring up an elaborate rhetoric where *ghammâz* (a wink; another name given to the tattoo between the eyebrows) justifies our argument. The (rhetorical) inscription of the wink requires a rhythmic quality, the transport of the image starting a musical intercalation. In the wink, a delirious movement dominates: it appropriates the other and dissolves it. A banal fantasy, to be sure, the tattooed wink attempts flight, attempts a suspension of meaning. Tattoos are the "exercise of a backward glance."[64]

The gestural finds an explicit example in the word *raffâda* (that which supports; on the stomach) or in the shameless expression *wachma fûgû* (a tattoo *on top of*, meaning, on the pubis). The rhetoric loses all restraint in its respect for the rite of lovemaking. It's an imposed decorative invitation that makes a simple and untangled excitement bloom.

Another category is reserved for indicating either color, like *la-kḥal* (the black; on the cheek, substitute for a mole), or geometric designs, such as the *bu ʿarrûj* (the torturous or a broken line; on the chin). There's no relation between the name and the ornamentation; this is true of all geometric designs, which are often called by the name of a plant, flower, or animal. Among the plants are a palm tree, a cypress, and a lemon tree, or more precisely, *chaqat al-gar ʾa*, the cleft of a lemon tree, which is a V-shaped tattoo. Among the flowers, there is, unsurprisingly, *warda* (a rose; on the wrist or hand), the thorn of the rose being enchanted by the needle's tip. Among the animals, there might be, characteristically, *ḥniyyach* (a small snake) on the forearm. As we said earlier, there's absolutely no analogy between the name of the drawing and the representation; but, at the same time, this suggests a timely comparison to the body's jewels: the *khalkhâl* (either ring or toe ring) or, even more deliciously, the *salsâl el-fakhdayn* (thigh chain).

Here's an abridged list of the names of tattoos, which slides over different places on the body:[65]

1) Between the eyebrows
   - *ḥammâqa*: the fearful
   - *ghammâz*: that which winks
   - *t ʾaba ʾ*: stamp, seal
   - *t ʾallâha*: that which looks up
   - *d ʾallâl*: that which casts shadows
   - *bûja*: tattoo between the eyebrows
2) Cheek
   - *la-kḥal*: the black, a mole
   - *ljam sidi*: my master's bridle
3) Chin
   - *uchâm al-laḥya*: chin tattoo
   - *bu ʾ arrûj*: broken line, the tortuous
   - *jrîda*: palm tree

- *siyâla*: chin tattoo
- *tasnida d-Lalla Fatima Zahra*: consecration to Lalla Zahra, daughter of the Prophet Muhammad

4) Chest
   - *sdar*: chest
5) Back
   - *ḥamla*: burden, pregnancy
6) Shoulder
   - *'awwâma*: that which swims
7) Arm
   - *usâda*: pillow
8) Forearm
   - *ḥniyyach*: small snake
9) Wrist or hand
   - *khalkhâl*: toe ring
   - *khatam slimaniya*: seal of Solomon
   - *warda*: rose
10) Stomach
   - *ḥammâqa*: the fearful
   - *raffâda*: that which supports
   - *wachma fûgû*: pubic tattoo
11) Thigh
   - *salsäl al-fakhdayn*: thigh chain
12) Knee, leg, foot
   - *khalkhâl al-fakhdayn*: toe ring
   - *qat'at al-wâd*: river crossing

The way that tattoos are named draws its variations from general rhetoric (popular culture) in a double text (of drawing and naming) whose movement migrates between different semiotic systems: tattoos, rugs, jewelry. The intersemiotic gesture is an erotic transport, a production of meaning that rotates out from a minimal geometric sign, a color, or a movement of the body. A lesson in modesty is learned from this unveiled mise-en-scène where the loss of meaning is the risk of a craft (writing) often initiated in ravishment, in a wink, in a grafted written mark.

What's general rhetoric? We can conceive of it as a signifying (intersemiotic) production that plays out in three registers: the letter, the graphic, and the musical. To mark correspondence, as Jakobson did, between a grammatical composition and a geometric composition is useful,[66] but as in Mallarmé's work, we would have to generalize the points of correspondence, make each paradox of their slippage explode, and intensify the intertextual unraveling.

Necessarily inside language, a ceaselessly oblique polyphonic reading, which is both floating and mad with pleasure, would dedicate itself to bringing the meaning of repressed semiotic systems to light.

Annex IV

Schemas for Moroccan Tattoos

The following schemas for Moroccan tattoos are inspired mostly by the documents of Joseph Herber, published in *Hespéris* (see figures 2.8–14).

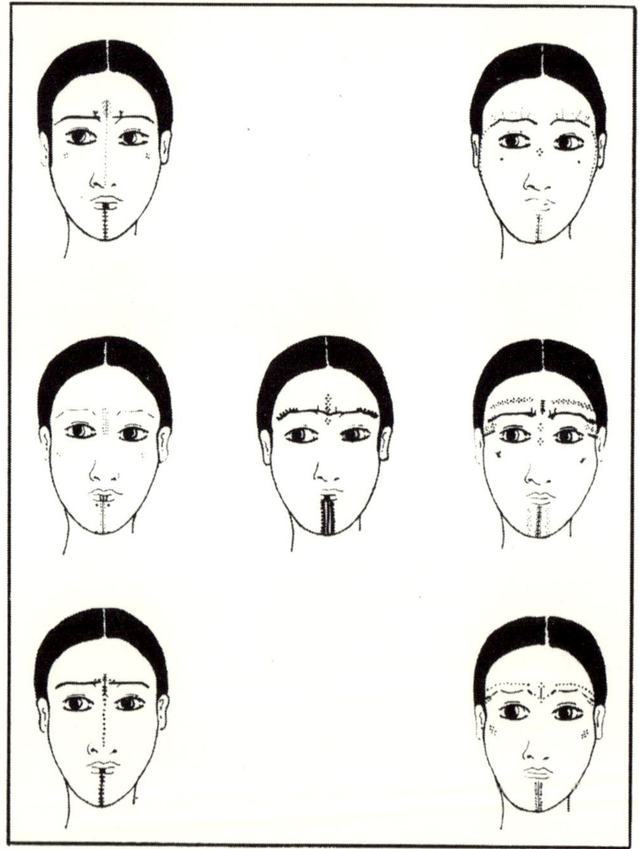

Figures 2.8–14. Schemas for Moroccan Tattoos (Corpus).

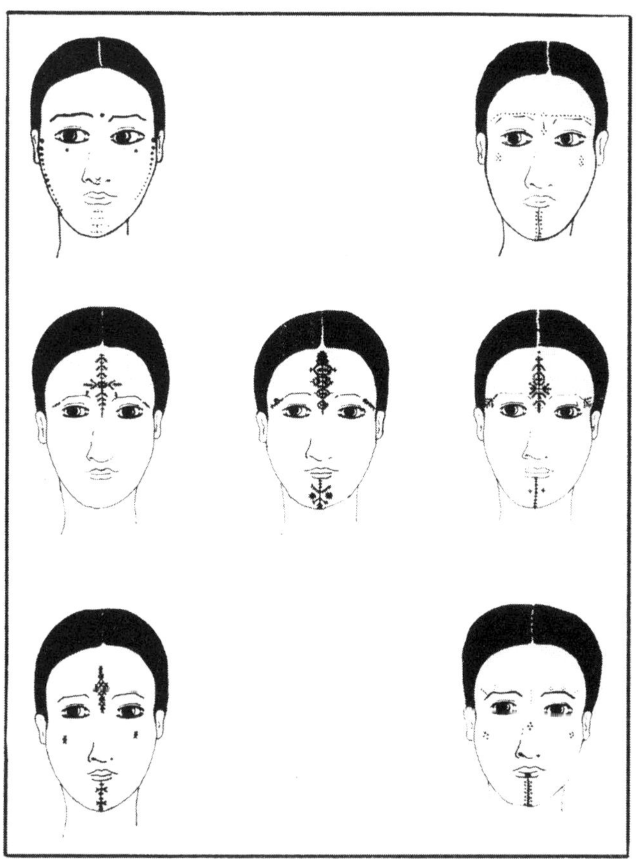

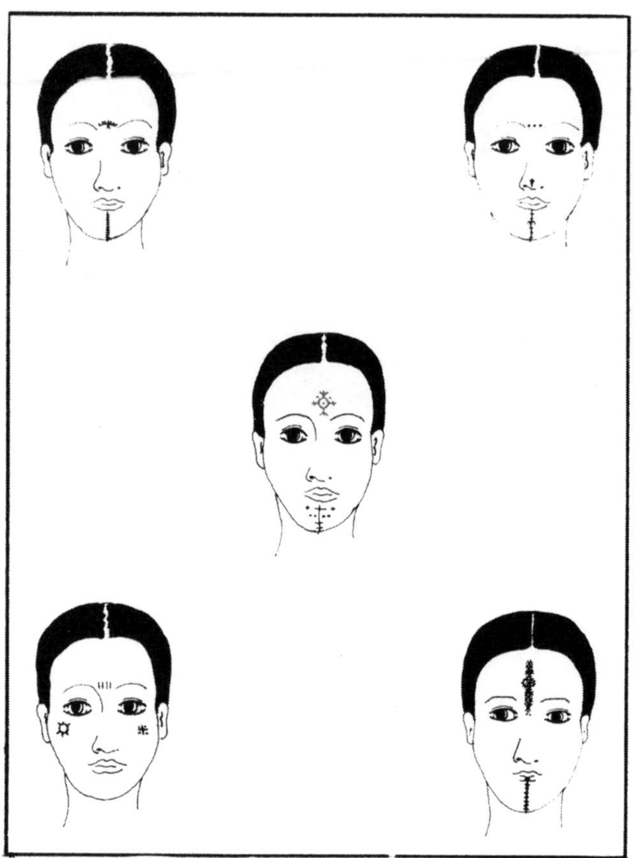

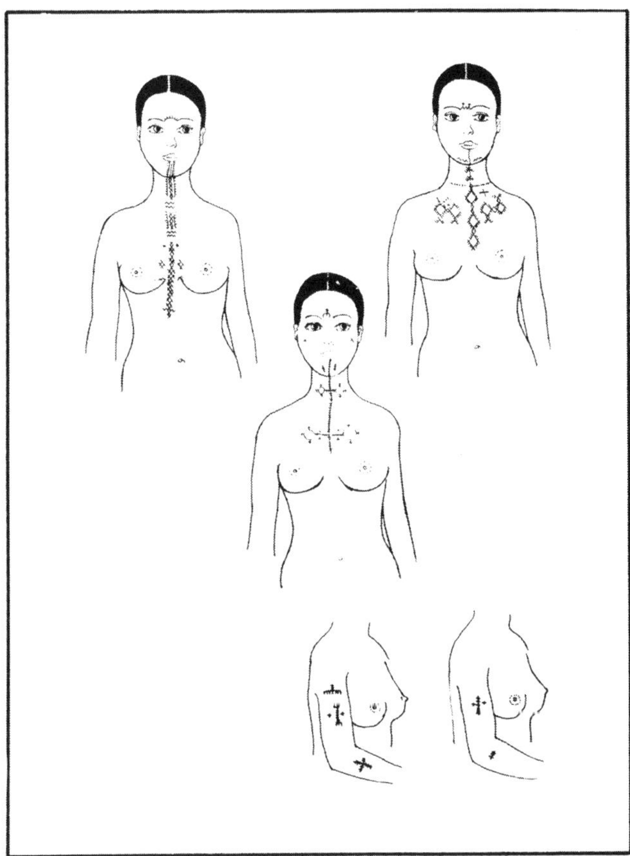

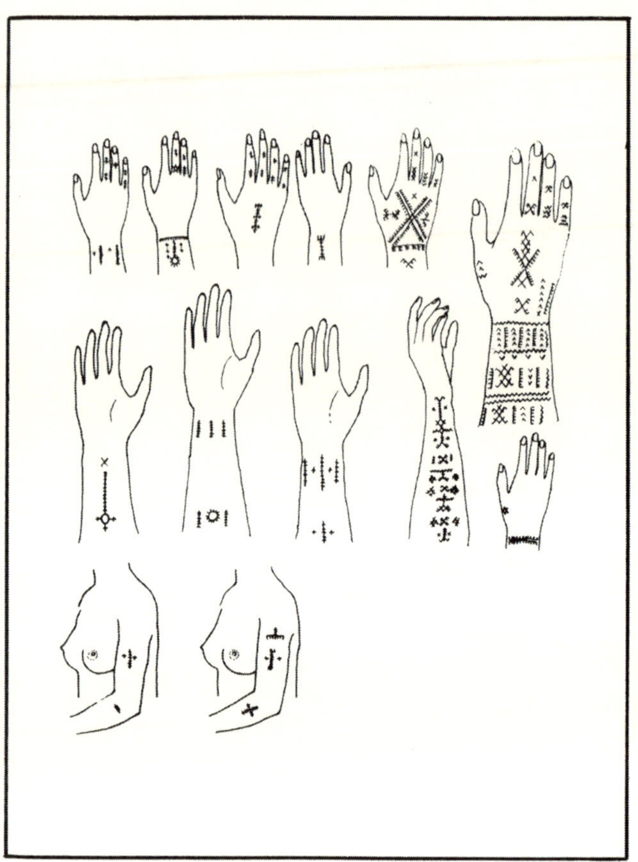

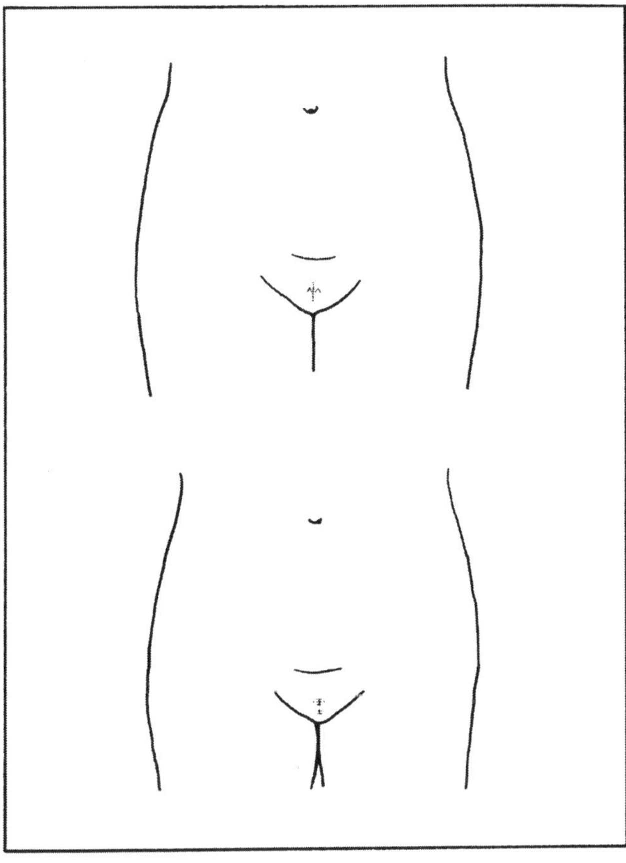

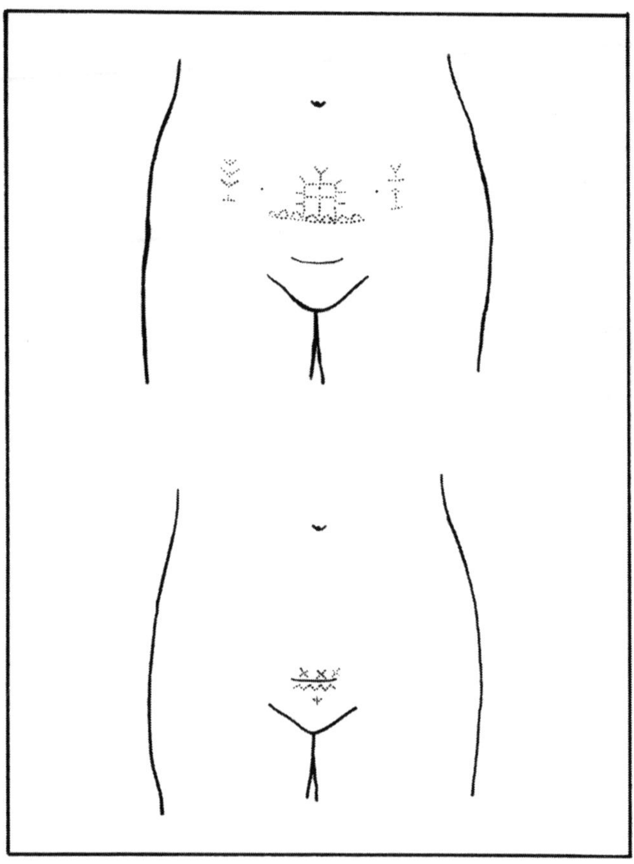

The Tuaregs use an alphabet called *tifinagh* (twenty-four letters). The characters are derived from the ancient Libyan writing system (see figure 2.15).

Some signs in ancient Moroccan tattoos are also found in tifinagh. Similarly, some signs are used in both tattooing and animal branding.

alphabet touareg	valeur
⦶ ◫	b
]⊏	f
+	t
+∃	ṭ
Π	d
∃	ḍ
⊙ ⊡	s
ⵣ	z
#	ẓ
Ɔ	š
I	j
||	l
○ □	r
·:	k
⋈	g
Ṫ	ǧ
∷	ḫ
⋮	ġ
⋯	q
⁞	h
⊐	m
|	n
:	u, w
≶	i, y

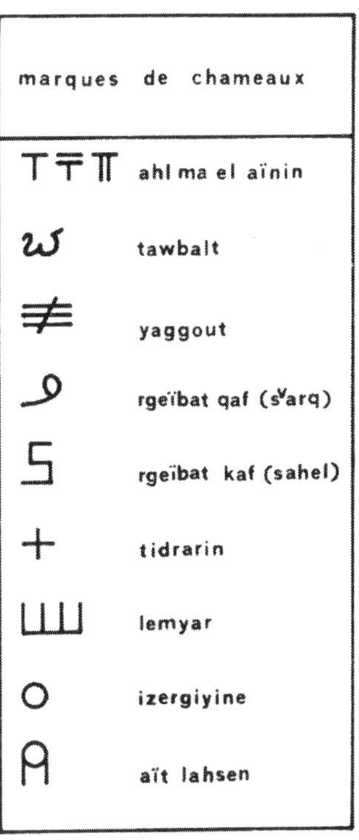

marques de chameaux	
T T̄ Π	ahl ma el aïnin
ω	tawbalt
≠	yaggout
ɔ	rgeïbat qaf (s̆arq)
5	rgeïbat kaf (sahel)
+	tidrarin
⊔⊔	lemyar
○	izergiyine
ᑎ	aït lahsen

Figure 2.15. Tuareg Alphabet.

Chapter 3

The Rhetoric of Lovemaking

1. Reading Note (Part I)

According to Cheikh Nafzawi, reading the Qur'an gets you ready for sex. We accept this divine postulate word for word, and we do so joyously; the proposed game to come will be to pervert the religious reading to lead it astray, and to turn it into hilarious laughter and the violence of lovemaking. The Qur'an is an aperitif of a ritual text, a pretext for sex. It announces sex, disfigures sex, makes the whirlwind of words and their variations float. The eroticism of our cheikh finds its wings, like a scared bird, in this airy suspension.

How is it possible to make love after God's benediction, after his words? The cheikh responds methodically, with many medical and pedagogical arguments. But what's admirable is the exquisite rhetorical transport, the theatric transformation of a simple pedagogical exercise into a veritable eroticism.

The Perfumed Garden for the Pleasure of the Spirit, the work under analysis here, isn't exactly a pornographic text—at least as far as such things are understood in the West, that's to say, as dirty, desacralized texts fueled by the crude rhetoric of ejaculation: the ejection and absorption of sperm. That type of pornography repeals the erotic—at least if we agree with Roland Barthes, who says that

> the pornogram [is] a new chemistry of the text, it is the fusion (as though under high temperature) of discourse and body . . . , to that, that point having been reached, the writing will be what regulates the exchange of Logos and Eros, and that it will be possible to speak of the erotic as a grammarian and of language as a pornographer.[1]

Only in this context is it possible to call our cheikh a pornographic writer.

But it isn't a question of a Muslim Sade, who could fundamentally subvert the doxological and social order. *The Perfumed Garden* is addressed to a symbolic vizier, and the author continuously claims the authority of divine discourse; moreover, the rhetoric of the text is classical, sometimes vulgar. It's a rhetoric of order and law, no doubt, but grabbed by the horns, exaggerated in its basic terms. In this way, an assumed divine taxonomy achieves a surprising reversal of images and meaning.

Who is making love, then? To be carried out systematically, fornication requires long preparation, the conjuration of many texts, to wit, a generalized grammar, by which gesture, graph, and perfume measure and dissolve each other in a floating signification, mad with pleasure. Fornication is asceticism that is as rigorous and delirious as mysticism; it's a complex enunciation of the licit and the forbidden, a rotation of signs divinely hierarchizing the body. To make love rigorously and in a delirious manner is the very movement of truth.

There is, then, no comparison to the Marquis de Sade, not even in erotic technique: our cheikh is silent on the practice of sodomy and fellation. There are some quick allusions to female homosexuality (which he denounces) and to dreams of incest. Like Freud, he uses wordplay, but he doesn't come to the same interpretations that psychoanalysis does. Moreover, he limits himself to two quickly sketched examples of bestiality. Rather, for our cheikh, the point is to teach the reader how to systematically conduct licit male-female sex. Nafzawi's combinatorics is limited by divine decree: orgies are fantasies that seize upon differences in social class; it is always slaves who engage in group sex with their mistresses. A ritual orgy cements the relation of master to slave.[2] It's metaphysical subterfuge once again. The hoped-for displacement is more modest in Nafzawi than in Sade, but it is strategically jubilant; it's a system at once divine and libertine.

The construction of *The Perfumed Garden* is an irradiance, a felted interlacing of three principal codes: a doxological code, a narrative code, and a symbolic code. The doxological code (the Word of God) inaugurates the text and seals its end; its presence is visible in vivifying snippets of poetry. It is, in sum, the voyeuristic code, regulating the discursive scene: a strategic node, it controls delirium and the wobble of the text. It's the explicit voice of the law, the breath by which the human being makes divine love. To get a woman pregnant, it's necessary—according to the rules of the game—to penetrate a cosmic space with the power of lovemaking. And this breath is spoken through a chant: assonance and rhymed prose (chajʿ) are witnesses of a grace inscribed musically in the body. Being of a metaphorical (or parabolic) nature, the Qurʾanic citation lends itself to the full bandwidth of hermeneutic jubilation; a flagrant arbitrariness delimits its interventions because the citation is an inscription whose origin is named, necessary, total, anterior to every code, every word.

The *narrative code* is that of the story, of the anecdote; it's regulated by the ritual word of the conversation and the circulation of mythic time, and, functionally, it illustrates a lesson or develops an erotic argument. For example, when he speaks of the treachery of women, Nafzawi recalls an orgy of Blacks and royal women, including the queen. The movement of the narrative recalls the orgy, that's to say, the systematic practice of a fantasy. In the orgiastic scene, the narrative obeys a circular economy of exchange:

one erection is exchanged for another; one ejaculate for another; one act of lovemaking for a poem; one piece of property for its simulacrum; one jealous fury for a decapitated head. . . . Although it's often ornamented with a dull or tautological rhetoric, the narrative lays bare all that the signification implies, unseating and reorienting all codes. It's the fantasy that determines how luxury, perfume, rhythm, and the inscribed graph touch the body. Its transformation only obeys the scene of delirium; the syntax only obeys the phrasing of lovemaking violence.

What we call the symbolic code is all the motifs of interpretation: the rhetoric of wordplay, the theological or scientific exegesis, the reading of dreams—in short, Nafzawi's erotic ideology. What's remarkable in Nafzawi is the text's modernity, although it dates from the sixteenth century. Every semiotic system is a syntactic and lexical combinatorics; it's clear that this is plain to Nafzawi, since he doesn't even mention it. We're granted access to a semiotic sketch, whose analogical level is based on a movement of jubilation: the rhetoric of lovemaking is compared to that of culinary matters; perfume, to the violence between Logos and Eros; ejaculation, to wordplay; overcoming the space-time dichotomy, to a rotation of orgiastic scenes. So many vertiginous examples that "turn" (as milk is churned) the semiotic theories of our time on their head.

The cheikh's text has a rare quality (which is why it's popular): its simple language reduces the distance between oral literature and written literature (of the elites), and Nafzawi's science is based on the home remedies of the medicine of the masses. The differences between the social classes aren't effaced; all our cheikh has at his disposal to alleviate these differences is wordplay. Sex is necessary, as is the divine word; the one and the other are pleasures that can't be subsumed under the appropriation of one person by another. From the Qur'anic parable to the jubilation of sex, everything is annulled. All that is left is an all-knowing God.

Fortunately for *The Perfumed Garden*, Nafzawi's biography remains enigmatic. We don't know if he wrote other texts. *The Perfumed Garden* was probably written around A.H. 925 (1523 C.E.). While Cheikh Sidi Muhammad Nafzawi was born in Nafzawa (in southern Tunisia), he lived in Tunis. According to legend, when the bey of Tunis asked him to become a qadi, our cheikh, not daring to refuse, asked for some time to consider the offer: it was a ruse that allowed him to adroitly delay the appointment, during which time he wrote (or finished writing) this text. This legend is accompanied by an anecdote as well, recounted by the cheikh himself in the introduction to *The Perfumed Garden*. There, he states that *The Perfumed Garden* was preceded by the writing of a little book, which he simply called *The Universal Flame*. The grand vizier of Tunis had asked for Nafzawi and shown him a copy of it. The cheikh was ashamed; he trembled. But the vizier calmed him down, telling him that the text had a ring of truth to it, then asking him to add several chapters on sex medicine. These two short texts indicate the distant attitude of our cheikh with regard to authority and his pleasure in having written *The Perfumed Garden*: "This act of witnessing is one I will keep next to my heart for the day of Judgment."[3]

The final text is made up of twenty-one chapters. To avoid retranslating the text, I relied almost exclusively on the translation of the staff caption Baron de . . . (in an edition from 1876, which saw no more than thirty-five copies published).[4] This translation was then modified by a doctor de L . . . , then by a third person; the publisher informs us that the work was interrupted by the third person's death. The notes on the final text are a veritable Borgesian palimpsest, and the publisher takes pains to repudiate the remarks of one or another of the translators, all three, and even the author of *The Perfumed Garden* himself. In short, these editorial footnotes constitute a parallel text. As for illustrations, there are drawings and paintings that all in all constitute a series of madcap delights.

Only a number of twists and turns have kept this publication from my attention: there are other translations in French and in English, but the French translations have all been suppressed. The Arabic version is sold everywhere in the Arabic-speaking world at a modest price. The 1876 French edition has been banned in Morocco for more than fifteen years simply because it belongs to a private library that is itself sequestered. The Bibliothèque nationale de France has placed *The Perfumed Garden* in a special collection: hell. Consulting it would take asking for permission from hell's gatekeeper, who would refuse you. Through my own means, however, I was able to get my hands on that wonderful translation, whose archaic phrases I have kept in certain cases. The excerpts below are evidently selections, inscribed in the fields of our dreams and fantasies. The subheads are my own.

2. *The Perfumed Garden* (Excerpts)

Erection Length

To bring pleasure to women, erections must be no more than twelve finger lengths, that's to say, three fists; and at least six finger lengths, or a fist and a half.

There are men whose erections are twelve finger lengths, or three fists; others are ten finger lengths, or two and a half fists; and still others are eight finger lengths, or two fists. The man whose erection is less than that can't please women.

Ideal Woman

The lower part of the stomach will be large; the vulva will be prominent and fleshy where the pubic hair sprouts all the way back to the butt; the vagina will be straight, not damp at all, soft and warm to the touch, emitting a strong heat outside, and without the odor of rotten eggs; her thighs will be strong, as will her butt. This woman will possess pendulous breasts; her waist will be curvaceous; her hands and feet will be remarkably elegant; her arms will be fleshy, as will her forearms; and her shoulders will be broad.

If you see a woman like this from the front, you're fascinated; if you see her from behind, you're ready to faint. Seated, the woman is a rounded dome; bending over, she's a sumptuous bed; and standing, she's the fringe of a flag.

The Woman to Avoid

Her vulva is large and cold, giving off an odor worse than that of carrion; she has no pubic hair; her flesh is pasty white; and her clitoris is heavy, tough, stinky, and damp.

Movements

First movement: the pail in the well. The man and the woman embrace after the man's erect penis is inserted into the woman, then the man thrusts once, then withdraws a little; the woman tries to find it again with a push forward, then she moves back as well. The man quickly initiates the movement again, and they continue like this, making sure to match the other's rhythm. They take care to put their feet against the other person's feet, hands against hands, and they move like a pail in a well.

Second movement: mutual shock. Each moves backward after the insertion of the erect penis but not so much that it comes all the way out, then they push together while embracing. They continue like that, pushing and pulling.

Third movement: finding a balance. The man thrusts normally, as he pleases, then he stops; the woman, keeping the erect penis in place, moves as the man did, until she wants to stop; then the man starts again. They continue until they ejaculate together.

Fourth movement: the size of love. With the part of his penis that he hasn't stuck inside the vagina, the man thrusts suddenly, like a sharp blow, and plunges his penis deep into the vagina. This is the same movement as that of a needle in the hands of a steady seamstress, who, after having plunged the needle into the fabric, removes it brusquely all the way to the thread's end. This is the example that the man and woman should follow. This movement works only for those men and women who can delay their ejaculation according to their will.

Fifth movement: vulva toothpicks. The man sticks his erect penis into the outer layers of the vulva, then explores them up, down, to the left, and to the right. Only a man with a very stiff erection can manage this movement.

Sixth movement: love fugue. The man sticks his erect penis completely into the vagina, to the extent that the pubic hairs of each partner are glued together tight and fast. Then, in that position, the movement must be energetic without allowing the penis to retract even a little. This is the very best movement. Women like it better than any other, because the head of the erect penis touches their G-spots. This is the movement that best satisfies the woman.

Position

It is said that there are women who can lie down with men and, while on their backs, raise one of their legs vertically into the air. On their foot, they place a lit lamp full of oil. The women can't let a single drop of oil fall, nor the lamp, which must also remain lit.

Economy of Sperm

Just as butter, full of cream, represents the quintessence of milk and just as milk, when the cream is skimmed off, loses its good qualities, so too is sperm formed from the quintessence of a man's food. Its loss debilitates the economy.

Kissing

Kissing must be audible. Its prolonged, gentle sound will be made from the movement between the tongue and the edge of the palate, wet with saliva. It will be produced by the movement of the tongue inside the mouth, as well as by the sharing of saliva, which will provoke the sound of suction.

Kissing on the exterior lips, producing a loud sound the likes of which we call "smooches," makes for no pleasure at all. This type is reserved for kissing kids and hands.

Kissing Poem

Languorous looks
Put one soul in communication with another
And tender kisses
Are go-betweens for the penis and the pussy.

Different Names for an Erection

ad-dakar

This word means "the male" for any creation; it also means "mention" and "memory." If a man has an accident that affects his ability to have an erection or if his penis is cut off, and if the man is therefore unable to fulfil his conjugal duty, it is said that "his erection has died"; that is, the erection (*dakr*) has become a memory (*dikr*) for the man.

al-ayr (from the word *al-kayr* [?])

In short, if we reflect the letter *kâf* (*k*) so that it appears backward, we get the word *al-ayr*.

ḥamâma (dove)

The penis is called this because it swells and, right when it begins to detumesce, looks like a white dove resting on its eggs (*bayd* = eggs and testicles).

al-harmâq (the indominable)

When it swells into an erection, the penis begins to move its head, seeking restlessly to penetrate the vagina, which it enters roughly, with insolence and without asking for permission.

az-zab (the erection)

This word comes from the word *dab* (crawling). This name is given to the erection because it appears between the women's thighs, sees the fleshy vulva, begins to crawl over the thighs toward the pubis, then approaches the entrance (of the vulva), continues to crawl into position, and finally, when it's in the right position, penetrates into the middle of the vagina to ejaculate.

fadlâq (the liar)

The penis gets this name because of its ruses and subterfuges. Approaching the woman, it sits up and seems to say to the vulva, "Today, my desires will find their home in you, O friend!" And the woman, seeing it thus, is shocked by its size and seems to say, "Who could ever receive such a large penis?" To answer, it puts its head at the vulva's door, opens the gates, and penetrates deeply. When it starts to move around inside, the woman disdains it and says, "You move around like a liar!" Because it won't be inside for long, the two testicles seem to say, "Our dick is dead! It dies right after jouissance!" Rapidly withdrawing from the vulva, the dick tries to raise its head again but falls limp and inert. The testicles repeat, "Our brother is dead! Our brother is dead!" The dick protests, "Hardly!" But the vulva shouts, "Where are you going? O liar, you said that once you entered, you'd stay forever!"

az-zaddâm (the digger)

The penis gets this name from how, when it meets a vulva that doesn't want to be penetrated immediately, it burrows a passage with its head, breaking and tearing everything like a wild animal in rut.

al-khayyat' (the tailor)

The penis gets this name from how it only enters the vagina after having roved around at its door like a needle in a tailor's hand, grabbing and rubbing to the point that it's suitably inflamed. Then it enters.

al-kharrat' (the swirler)

This name was given to the penis that arrives at the vulva's door as though it has something urgent to communicate, knocks on the door, swirls about all sides—with neither shame nor shamelessness, pursuing its investigations to the right, to the left, forward, and backward—then, suddenly, penetrates with the speed of an arrow deep into the vagina, where it ejaculates.

al-'awwâm (the swimmer)

This is the penis that, when it penetrates the vulva, doesn't choose one spot over any other but rather starts to turn—to the right and to the left, forward and backward, mostly in the middle—and to swim around, moving between the sperm that it shoots out and the liquid that the vagina secretes as though, scared of drowning, it's trying to escape death.

al-a'war (the one-eyed)

Because the penis only has one eye, which doesn't resemble other eyes or see clearly.

abû-al-'ayn (the one with an eye)

The penis got this name because its one eye is one of a kind: it doesn't have a pupil or eyelashes.

al-bakkây (the crier)

This name was given to the penis because of the copious tears it sheds. As soon as it becomes erect, it cries. When it sees a woman, it cries. When it sees a fatty white vulva, it cries. When it touches a woman, it cries. Even thoughts of sex move it to tears.

abu-lu-'âba (the spitter)

The penis got this name because, when approaching the vulva, it starts to salivate, and its eye starts crying. This crying is especially copious when it hasn't made love for quite a while; tears will even be shed on clothes.

This penis is very common, and there are few men who are not gifted in this manner.

al-hattâk (the smasher)

This is the rough-and-ready penis that gets hard fast and stays erect like a baton or a bone. Its name comes from how blood flows through it in abundance and from how it tears the veil of the vulva of virgins, making its blood flow.

al-murkhi (the flaccid)

This penis can never enter because it's too limp; it's limited to rubbing around the mouth of the vulva until ejaculation. This gives no pleasure to women because it enflames their passion without satisfying it, making women grouchy and irritable.

al-mukchif (the discoverer)

This penis is familiar with every aspect of lovemaking: it has a deep knowledge of the vagina's changing humidity, freshness, dryness, tightness, or heat.

Different Names for a Woman's Sex

al-farj (cleft, opening, passageway, all the female sex organs)

The word *faraj* means "deliverance from misfortune."

al-kass (the vulva)

A very fleshy and round vulva with long lips. This vulva has a big cleft, its perfectly symmetrical lips spreading wide, with a prominent opening. It is without a doubt the most pleasant, the best of all. May God grant each man the chance to taste such a vulva! Amen!

ar-rahmûn (the libidinous)

Name given to the vulva of a young virgin.

al-'ass (the primitive)

Name given to all, no matter what.

az-zarzûr (the starling)

The vulva of a young woman and, to our knowledge, of a brown-haired woman.

ach-chaq (the cleft)

The vulva of a skinny woman. It's like a crack in a wall, and there's no sign of flesh. May God guard us against it! Amen!

abû-t'art'ûr (the one that has a "crest," meaning clitoris)

This is the name of the vulva that has a red crest like a rooster's, which pops out high and wide during lovemaking.

abû-khuchîm (the pug-nosed)

The vulva with thin lips and a little tongue. (Translator's note: lips = labia minora; tongue = clitoris.)[5]

al-qanfûd (the heron)

This is the vulva of an old, haggard woman, when, due to her advanced age, her skin becomes disgusting and her pubic hair few and far between.

as-sakutî **(the taciturn)**

The vulva that never speaks. Even if the penis would enter a hundred times a day, the vulva would say nary a word and would rest happy, looking on in absolute silence.

ad-dakâk **(the grinder)**

The vagina that grinds against the penis. As soon as the erect penis is inserted, this vagina has the habit of grinding to the left and to the right, searching for jouissance and trying to get the penis to hit the G-spot. It does so in such a way that, if it were possible, this vagina would swallow the testicles.

at'-t'aqîl **(the importunate)**

Here, the roles are reversed: the penis is pursued, and the vulva is the pursuer.

al-fachfâch **(the watering can, the detumescence)**

The vulvae of women who, when they cum, release from their orifices a very loud and echoey noise.

abû-jabha **(the one with a forehead)**

Some women have this vulva, which is very large and has a prominent pubis that forms something like a large, fleshy forehead.

al-'arîd' **(the large)**

The name given to the vagina of a fat, fleshy woman. When this woman crosses her legs, her vagina projects between her thighs like a baby cow's head; when she uncrosses her legs, it looks like a shaft of wheat placed between her thighs; when she walks, its undulating movements are visible underneath her clothes with each step. May God, in his goodness and generosity, not deprive us of a vagina like this! Amen!

al-maq'ûr **(without bottom, the holy)**

A vagina that goes on forever, which means that the G-spot is located in the depths.

abû-'ankara **(the hunchback)**

This vulva has a hard, prominent mons veneris, which extends out like the hump on a camel's back and extends back between the thighs like the head of a baby cow. May God allow us the pleasure of such a vulva! Amen!

al-mudî **(the vault)**

A large vagina, surrounded by dry and fleshy sides that are rounded into the shape of a vault and composed of a hard, compact mass of fat. May God protect us from it!

al-masbûl **(the long)**

A vulva of this sort extends between the thighs from the pubis to the anus, looking like a magnificent long cucumber.

al-mulqî **(the duelist)**

Motivated by a violent desire for sex, some vulvae throw themselves with avidity toward the approaching penis, opening their mouths like a baby nearing its mother's breast. These vulvae also advance and retreat in front of the penis so as to position it directly in front of the G-spot, fearing that it would never make it there otherwise. The vulva and the penis are like skillful duelists: each time one of them rushes its adversary, the other raises its shield to parry and fend off the attack. The penis is represented by a sword, the G-spot by a shield. The one who ejaculates first is the vanquished, and the one who can delay ejaculation the longest is the vanquisher. And, to be sure, it's a beautiful combat! This is how I would wish to fight, to the death!

al-musaffaḥ **(the barred)**

This sort of vagina is rarely encountered. The defect that distinguishes it is sometimes natural; at other times, it results from a botched circumcision. In the wound's scar, a lump forms that bars entrance.

al-ladîd **(the delicious)**

A sample of the delights of heaven that God has sent to earth as a foretaste of those that await us, which are a thousand times better and inferior only to the life of the Generous One himself.

Epic

Abû al-Haylîy's penis remained erect
For thirty days thanks to onions.
Abû al-Hayjâ, for his part, deflowered in one night
Twenty-four virgins without breaking for food,
But first he had eaten his fill of chickpeas and drunk
Camel milk mixed with honey.
I'll never forget Maymûn, who, while having sex, was able
To cum for fifty straight days.
He was happy to be able to accomplish this task,
So much so that when ten more days were tacked on, bringing
His total to seventy days, he wasn't upset at all.[6]
Even if, during this period, he ate only egg yolks and bread.

Stories

The Woman and the Hunchback

The woman said to the hunchback, "When you want to hug, you can't; your hunchback's in the way. Your hard-on's mine. But the erection on your back, where am I supposed to put it?"

The Woman and the Ass

When it was time for the evening meal, the woman approached the ass, took off its saddle, and lay down on her back, placing the animal's hooves to the side of her body. Then, she took some of its shit and pee, which she mixed together and rubbed over her vulva. Then she got on all fours beside the ass, readying herself, her vulva directly in front of the animal. The ass approached, smelled the vulva, and, thinking it had found a beast of burden, leaped onto her. As soon as she saw this, she grabbed its dick with her hand and put its head into her vulva's opening. The penis grew and grew until the erection filled her vagina and caused her to cum.

Dreams

If you see your erection cut off in a dream, you will soon die. This symbolizes the end of your happiness and the extinction of your race.

If you dream of *qusbûr* (coriander), that means that a vulva (*kass*) is healed (*barâ*).

He who dreams of a vulva (*farj*) will know: if he's sad and upset, God will free him; if he's poor, he'll become rich—because *farj* with an added vowel is the distancing of evil (*faraj* = deliverance). Likewise, if he's in debt, his debts will be forgiven.

But the best possible dream is to see an open vagina. Whether you can see deep inside or not, assuming the entrance is still open, know that success is soon to meet you where until now you've only met obstacles and that this turn in fortune will come from the intercession of someone entirely unexpected.

Generally, a bloody vulva is a sign of lovemaking, and the man who sees himself making love in his dream, all the way up to ejaculation, will succeed in everything. Our hypothesis is that the man who sees himself making love to a woman will get from her everything that he desires.

He who sees himself making love to people forbidden by religion, like his mother, his sister, etc. (all *al-rhâm*), must take from this dream that he will travel to the holy sites (*muḥarram*) and that, perhaps, he will even go to the house of God, the Sanctified (*bayt al-ḥarâm*), where he will see the tomb of the Prophet.

Seeing *sirwâl* (pants) is the sign of being appointed to an honorable position (*wilâyâ*) because of how, through vowel exchange, the two words *sir* (go) and *wâli* (named) mean "go return to your job."

Seeing a pair of pants in your dream is also a sign of protection for your "natural" parts, and it presages success in business.

Seeing windows and shoes in dreams is related to women. Effectively, when the erection penetrates the vagina, the vulva looks like either a window, through which the man passes his head to look around, or a shoe being put on. Accordingly, the man who sees himself in his dream either going through a window or putting on a shoe knows, if the shoe is new or in good shape, that a young woman or a virgin will soon be his; but the woman will be old if the shoe is old or scuffed and worn. In short, the woman's age is directly related to the decrepitude or newness of the window and shoe.

How to Cook for Sex

He who eats egg yolks (without the whites) on an empty stomach every day will find restless energy for lovemaking. The same is true for the man who, for three days, eats egg yolks with minced onions.

He who boils asparagus, fries it in fat, then covers it with egg yolks and spices—and who eats this dish every day—will be primed for lovemaking; this food stimulates sexual desire.

He who peels onions and puts them in a pot with condiments and herbs, then fries them in oil and raw egg yolks, will find in himself, after eating this food for several days, a vigor for lovemaking that surpasses all conception.

When drunk regularly, camel milk mixed with honey lends the man an unheard-of vigor during lovemaking, and it doesn't let the erection down—day or night.

He who eats eggs cooked with cinnamon and pepper for several days will see his sexual energy redouble. His erection will become entirely stiff and will seem to refuse to return to its normal state.

He who wants to make love all night long—and whose desire, which has come over him suddenly, does not allow him to make any preparations or follow any of the regimes I have just mentioned—should proceed in the following manner: Buy a large quantity of eggs, enough to be satiated, and have them fried in a pot with fresh fat and butter; once they're cooked, immerse the eggs in honey and mix. Eat as much of this as possible, with a little bit of bread, and rest assured that the erection won't droop for even a second the whole night long.

Last Recommendations

Lend me your ear and listen to the moans and cries of the woman; these are what bear witness to the violence of the pleasure you have given her.

Our recommendation is to not look inside the vagina because such a view can lead to blindness. This recommendation is scientific, not legal.

Also, avoid silk clothes: silk kills sexual desire.

Pornographic Books

Across all times and in all places, men—the important and the unimportant, the rich and the poor—like pornography, which is as essential for the soul as is the philosopher's stone for transforming ordinary metals into gold.

3. Reading Note (Part II)

The Book of Perfumes

Thought to be of divine essence,[7] perfume is the very thing of aphrodisiacal fervor: dry, hot, incorruptible by nature and language, it's the evanescent, ineffable mask of lovemaking violence. And it's because the aromatic series (as is said in the language of chemistry) introduces a drunken discontinuity into pleasure that perfume is, literally, a vertigo of sensations and meaning. It's against such a brutal discontinuity that perfume, by evaporating, inscribes into the hollows of the body the simulated sign of a sophisticated death. Perfumed death is an art of living, a perversion of the representation of true death. What could be more formidable than exquisite death, riveted to the trembling of the flesh? What could be more jubilant than an evanescent code that can be combined, rigged, perverted?

Nafzawi's rhetoric is undoubtedly aware of this subtle combination, which infiltrates a chain of correspondences and oppositions. Describing the good and bad vulva, the good and bad vagina, our cheikh systematizes oppositions: perfumed/putrid, hot/cold, fleshy/skinny—the good being on the side of the gardens of Arabia, and the bad on the side of decomposition (corrupted egg, rotting carcass, sweating clitoris).

No originality sparks anymore; these images are known to each person already "in perfume." Since ancient times, men have known the overwhelming power of perfume, associated with sacrificial rites, aphrodisiacal food, and cuisine in general. The Greek mythology of spices can be seen wonderfully in the myth of Adonis: this beautiful adolescent—at once effeminate, androgynous, and sterile (Epictetus calls him a "twig without knots"[8])—is the lover of Aphrodite (i.e., sensual pleasure embodied, who was "so proud of the power of desire"[9]) and the son of Smyrna (Myrrha), who seduced her father without his being aware. (To gently punish her, Theias transforms her into the myrrh tree.) Adonis—the irresistible lover adored by women during the Adonia festival, when the scene of their sensual disorder is recreated—is a perfume born of an incestuous act.[10]

Just like Myrrha's myth (the Greek word *μυρσίνη*, or "myrtle," can refer to the clitoris or the vulva), Adonis's myth reveals the radically perverse nature of perfume. Like perfume, lovemaking violence is a decorative dissolution of being, a volatile trace of bare death. Perfume coats the naked body, making it disappear. As for dreams, since Mallarmé is here, we say that perfume is "foam," through which the dancer's foot speaks to us.[11] Foam perfume: the limpid dispersion of our representation of death as the fragmentation of meaning.

The subtle Mallarmean variation implies a certain rhetoric of disappearance, dear to Baudelaire and Huysmans. Everything takes place as though the poetics of perfumes and spices, to conjure their power, returns their representation recursively to another code, closer to the perfumed universe but easier to grasp and less uncertain. By its nature, perfume makes the graspable, as well as property and possession, dissolve. This displacement often crystallizes around music, whose code originates in an equally subtle evanescence but whose degree of evanescence is less strong than that of volatile spirits. Both are marked by gyratory movement, but perfume and music are apperceived differently. Because it is an autonomous code, music is a cyclical chain of an unlimited sensual expansion. While perfume's movement—discontinuous, brutal, and violent—is a secret of sensual disorder, its gyration defies every musical code. It is sovereignty itself.

And that's not to say that perfume is without a code: there is, for instance, the chemical code of perfume making. What's transparent here is that perfume's code is always an element of another (culinary, medical, aphrodisiac) code. Its poetics displaces it forever in an analogical chain. Baudelaire writes,

> There are perfumes fresh as children's flesh,
> Soft as oboes, green as meadows,
> And others, corrupted, rich, triumphant,
>
> Possessing the diffusion of infinite things,
> Like amber, musk, incense and aromatic resin,
> Chanting the ecstasies of spirit and senses.[12]

Baudelaire's analogy conjures up the power of perfume, encircles the vertigo suggested by a return to other codes—especially to music. Huysmans didn't fear comparing perfume to languages.[13] It's clearly a metaphor. Does perfume obey a double articulation? There's no way to fully respond to this here. All that is possible to offer, somewhat arbitrarily, are some brief suggestions on the existence of perfumes. While of course coming directly from nature, aromatic plants left behind their splendid wildness quite early; in their earliest history, their use was linked to a division of work between men and women, it seems, with men dedicating themselves to hunting and women to cooking. The way we encode perfumes as feminine arrives from this period of pastoral-agricultural economy. This is a seductive hypothesis, which gives meaning and an archaic origin to this analogy between perfume and music. Perfume, however, has a stronger quality than the taboo, than incest (Adonis's); and music is a Dionysian joy stronger than life: although already torn to bits and buried, Orpheus's body lets escape, through the tomb, the final breath of transfiguration. Perfume and music inscribe on the body two poles in one single game. Here, to write is to institute in the hollows of the body a critical argument about transfiguration.

The historical origin of perfumes is unknown, but we can risk saying that the most ancient civilizations learned how to combine a series of spirits, essences, and perfumed aromas from aromatic plants.[14] They understood that these light, subtle bodies are gifted with a chemical, and surprisingly erotic and dangerous, power: perfume has the lethal force of poison. It's also not unsurprising that perfume is a node, a strategic point in the narratives of Cheikh Nafzawi, particularly in the story of the two prophets.

During the time of the Prophet Muhammad there was a man named Musaylima ibn Qays, a competing prophet, who mocked the revelations of the Qur'an, especially the sura "The Elephant":[15] "In the chapter 'The Elephant,' " he said, "I see the elephant. What's an elephant? What does it mean to be an elephant? What's a quadruped? A tail, and a tip of the tail, and a long nose. It's one of the creatures of our God the Magnificent! What else!"[16]

Musaylima also had a competitor, a female prophet named Sajah Tamimi,[17] who sent him a messenger, for the truth must win out! She proposed a debate so that they could settle who was on the side of the truth. Scared, he asked his tribesmen for advice. An old sage said to him, "Tomorrow morning, set up a tent full of multicolored brocades and decorated with furniture covered with all types of silk. Fill it with exquisite perfumes of all sorts, with ambergris, with musk, with all sorts of scents—rose, orange blossom, jonquil, jasmine, carnation, and other aromatic plants. When everything's ready, place golden pans filled with various perfumes inside the tent, like aloe vera, ambergris, and others. Afterward, fix the tent straps so that none of these perfumes can be smelled outside. Then, when you've noticed that their vapor has become intense enough to impregnate water, sit on your throne and send word to the prophetess that you're waiting for her and that she should come alone." Musaylima followed the old sage's advice, and when he sensed that the prophetess wanted to have sex, he sang her a poem, in which he asked which position she'd prefer. "Like this," she answered. "This is how the Prophet of God descends into me." After sex, she declared to her people that Musaylima was the bearer of truth. They married afterward.

Here, the narrative is an ever-expanding erotic sentence, knotted and unknotted according to the fugue-like movement of the riddle: Who owns the truth? Rhetoric is founded on a rigged exchange, since the vibratory pleasure is to regulate erotic sovereignty each time in an oblique blow. To read or retell a narrative is nothing other than to produce the outline of a false repetition: repetition being impossible, its gaming is nevertheless always a discourse about this impossibility.

In this brief story, truth is a sexual illusion but an illusion detailing in the production of its trace the calligrams of a transfiguration (which are, according to semioticians, the narrative's knots, or nodes). A transfiguration not just because a droplet of sperm (Nafzawi would have said a "tear" of sperm) can give birth to prophets and can reveal their truth but also because mysticism is a double movement: as a discourse that gives rise to delirium, it shatters everything; it makes all the universe's order and disorder spring from the body. The body is like milk, that is, a liquid capable of a disorderly expansion. To cook up sex, you have to produce butter, an eternally renewable economic surplus, because ejaculation feeds death's economy. It's God (the doxological code) that regulates this evacuation, this circulation of air and liquid, of sperm and the truth that can spring from it. Nafzawi's rhetoric insinuates itself into the irresistible act of ejaculation. Musaylima dirties the Qur'an's parable: he ejaculates through violent perfumes and ravishing fabrics onto space and time; he ejaculates onto the prophetess by a rotating poem and by sperm that carries the truth.

This universal ejaculation is regulated by a general economy and rhetoric. The characters are the agents of its circulation, and they can existentially be fooled by a playing card or a code: giving one in the place of the other. What's a character, then? It's an agent transfixed by the movement of lovemaking. Mocking the Qur'an, Musaylima turns irony into an erotic, Sibylline moment; he displaces the Eros/Logos relation in an unprophetic, human act. How could he do so? It's known that society accepts only one prophet at a time. Musaylima is burdened by a dissolution of his divine being: Logos is recuperated by irony, and Eros by fornication. According to this decisive argument, the scene is organized in a process of naturalization. The old sage's advice is a sleight of hand: he naturalizes truth by the evanescent violence of perfume and sex. Nevertheless, it's an ambivalent naturalization: perfume is supposed to inspire an uninterrupted ejaculation, the fantasy of an extreme dissolution. This is an ejaculation that we can put an end to only when we stand against the preeminence and the omnipotence of the word. A prophet of lovemaking truth is an idolator of the phallus, while a (true) prophet transcribes the divine breath in the parable. This is where Cheikh Nafzawi's interest in our (false) prophet comes from; he clearly knows that the truth doesn't go down this path, but he needs Musaylima in order to explore his own fantasy.

The order of lovemaking obeys a divine discourse, which is principally metonymic and fetishistic. It outlines an idolizing (patriarchal) moral. The Black man, the orgy's convener, addresses the women, "Your life lies in the erection, as does your death. Your vulva is your religion; and the penis, your soul." This is the source of the lexical abundance concerning sexual organs and, subsequently, of this mirroring of anecdotes and this fissured descendance of written texts. Nafzawi's narrative vacillates in this double gesture—from an epic or mythic movement that is commonly found in fairy tales to another that is broken, breathless, led on by irony and a rotating set of words in play, and cinched by a scream, a prayer, and an anodyne moral:

"May God grant us such a vulva! Amen!" or "May God preserve us from such a vulva! Amen!" The story is consumed by a divine noise.

Nafzawi's fable is organized against the fear of chaos, or unlimited ejaculation. That is why a strict, measured, rotating semiotic exchange is necessary. In the story of Bahloul and the Sultan's daughter, we see the exchange of a cloak for sex, sex for a poem, an erotic position for a rag covered in sperm; and in the rhythm of the exchange, each in turn is wiped by and wipes the other after sex. This exchange value has a name: barter, in which ripping is dissolved in an ecstatic autocracy, namely, that of Dorérame's ritual castration: "The Sultan had his nose and ears cut off, as well as his penis, which they put into his mouth. Then he was hung from the gallows."[18]

Penis/Breast

The order of lovemaking is that of an invasion directed by the man: to kiss, to bite, to suck, to invade. The erotic signs obey a sacred geometry: kissing must proceed from right to left, the penis must be held in the right hand, the man must withdraw from the woman from the right. This rightness is a symbol of good augurs. Ritual sex transforms the natural economy of sperm; it is an alchemy that unifies man and woman in the doxological body, an alchemy whose description is based upon an aqueous rhetoric: "The moist kiss / is worth more than quick sex." Or "Saliva . . . more pleasant than honey diluted in pure water." In this watery, aromatic space, a mirror doubles the sex act; it's the man who ejaculates milk, and it's the woman who sucks it in: "Her vulva seemed to pump the penis, as though it were sucking it, just like a baby sucks at the mother's breast."[19] Who is castrating whom? The penis/breast is the androgynous image that saves the meaning of ejaculation from disorder.

The penis isn't the equivalent of the vagina, which is a cosmic space where the play of the elements (air, water) is found: to kiss, to suck, to ejaculate is to tattoo a divine writing on the woman's body.

Procreational, patriarchal mysticism ardently declares its ambivalence; the penis/breast duo ardently veils the fear of absorption, from which is born the eternal myth of the ravenous vagina: Astarte, Aisha Kandicha.

Patriarchy

From beginning to end, the time allotted to lovemaking unfolds according to a strict combinatorics: choosing positions, adjusting or tossing aside the partner, moving, ejaculating together. What's a position in the patriarchal order? It's the gesture of an invasion, the choice deriving from an impossible appropriation of the other. Positioning is playing on the divine symmetry of the body while being fixed to a controlled displacement. A geometric motif or rhythm corresponds to each position, a presence that receives and endlessly names each sign. The body measures the economy of cyclical violence: "Lend an ear and listen to the woman's gasps and moans."

The positions sketched out by Nafzawi—for the most part inspired by Hindu eroticism—have delicious names: somersault, Archimedes's screw, the ostrich's tail, hunting the hunter, clinging to the toes, what butts see of each other, and so on, the metaphoric chain naming and redrafting the order of nature and that of the patriarchy.

The patriarchal ideology is, in the end, a mysticism of the transmission of being through blood and sperm. The sexual values that make it up (maximum procreation, virginity, and the woman's faithfulness) crystallize around her sex a delirious domination and a suspended taste for murder. If Scheherazade escapes death by reciting a story every night, it's because her words unknot the patriarchal delirium and transcend it through a novelesque consciousness: she shows how to *make* tales. "To die and to go beyond one's limits are exactly the same thing," Bataille writes.[20] In being dissolved into the Sultan's madness, Scheherazade's virginity leaves open a double writing: one cinched in patriarchal binding (blood, children, and the natural order return), and the other in a dispersion, an unheard-of expansion of stories that produces in us a mirroring of the erasure of values and patriarchal images. It's in this manifold figurative doubling that an erotic position knots and unknots, in the throes of a rigorous and often frenzied desire.

Tautology

In an Arab fairy tale, a princess establishes the following condition for her suitors: her husband will be the man who presents the poem that best paints the portrait of her body from head to toe. Several suitors set to work. The poet from al-Sham and the poet from Yemen meet to discuss. Each reads the other's poem. In the night, the Yemenite assassinates his rival. He goes to the palace and joins the competition. After reciting his poem, he is declared the winner. But, to everyone's surprise, the princess orders him killed on the spot. General uproar. The princess says, "The Yemenite's word choice was from the region of al-Sham. The Yemenite has killed my husband."[21]

We are led to believe that this lost poem contained two stanzas about the princess's vulva. This absence has a meaning: it indicates that beauty is indescribable. The disappearance and the disfiguration of the poem present the enigma of this impossibility. Without a doubt, beauty's language is tautological, but only if we move away from thinking about tautology as a linguistic phenomenon and consider it as materiality, a weightiness that can be opened—insidiously or in explicit violence—in the discursive order. Nafzawi's tautology plays over two levels: the first consists of a systematic naturalization in which the penis is a column; the woman's teeth are pearls; her eyes are roses; her lips are ebony; and her belly is "round like a cupola, . . . a belly button that looks like a pearl in the middle of a golden cup."[22]

This well-turned vessel of nothingness is broken, however, as if in shaping it, the tautology exploded the root of its immobility: "Her lips fresh and red like a blood-soaked sword."[23] The modest work of the tautology is to locate within the most derisory type of anonymity a subtle metamorphosis, an active and mocking game, relevant to our tendency to divide the world into two spheres: one endowed with meaning and the other without meaning. Then, the tautology can be a scriptural transfer. And it's in this way—between our amorphous space and writing's productive elan—that the tautology is torn, reversed: "God gave [the vulva] a mouth, a tongue, two lips; it looks like the gazelle's footprint in the desert sands."[24]

Dream Language

Just like every other text, Nafzawi's is a transformation achieved through two rhetorical modes: a minor one, which is that of every tautological language, as discussed above; and a major one constituting an irreducible movement in the symbolic chain toward a use value. This is a movement by which the generalized, universal exchange of signs creates the text and inaugurates the rotation of codes. Not only does our cheikh establish the status of the body as writing—"Her ebony eyebrows looked like the curved line of the letter *nūn*" (ن)[25]—but he anticipates a type of modernity by building an eroticism from the interpretation of the dream and from a zany substitution of words.[26]

In the end, Nafzawi's eroticism is a transformation of language and its hierarchy. Historically, it belongs to the type of mystical discourse that remains alive in popular culture: clairvoyance, geomancy, spells, predictive games derived from transparent bodies, animal bones, and bird auguries. A person must access a state where, as Ibn Khaldun states, "a veil is formed between the eyes and the mirror, which is like a cloud, where the images are seen that are the objects of perception."[27] The mystical sign works on a three-tiered language: the sign that chooses the elect and the inspired and that makes them speak (prophecy and angelism); the sign of clairvoyance by which presence is felt and named in a bolt of lightning, in no more time than needed to be revealed (inspiration and dreams); and finally the bodily sign, the animal space consigned to decomposition.

Nafzawi's rhetoric is based on the interstitial unveiling of the sign: God defines the erotic moral, the Prophet legitimizes it, and the writer transcribes it. This is the source of the usage of two revelatory processes: enigmatic discourse and the theater's stage. Here, the body is an inverted enigmatic discourse; a riddle or a theatrical set corresponds to each name for the penis or vagina: the name is the question of the riddle and the supreme signified, and the answer is the spacing and the dispersion of the signified itself—in such a way that the body is this very overdetermination of meaning, which is veiled, unveiled, made into theater, and breathed into life in the enigmatic chain.

In a cursory reading of *The Perfumed Garden*, a reader would be seduced by the excessive debauchery of the symbol. The divinatory games that work the text's language at its most irreducible level—that is, the graphic space of writing—must be taken seriously. To point to the phallus, all Nafzawi has to do is invert a letter (*al-ayr/al-kayr*) or substitute one vowel for another. At the same time, the meaning of the dream is suspended in a graphic drift, in a vocal inversion. Nafzawi didn't make such a discursive movement into a radical gesture; his work on language is combined with a descriptive realism that resists language's rubrics. This is no clearer than in his interpretation of dreams.

Freud said that everyone dreams in their own language. In the traditional typology, there are three sorts of dreams: "The reflection of one's thoughts and experiences that one has during wakefulness, what is suggested by Satan to frighten the dreamer, [and] glad tidings from Allah."[28] To dream is, as we say, to give voice to another realm of desire. Being, while dreaming, is the very movement of this sharing, this rupture. In revealing itself at night, the body becomes an angel and is transported into the euphoric vapor that sanctifies even incest: from the word *ar-ḥam*, Nafzawi produces an incestuous paradise through a play of mirrors. And while this revelation of the body is constructed in the dream, he cleverly creates the text. To have sex, to dream, to write—these activities are linked to the same movement: rhetorical transport and mystical vapor.

Chapter 4

The Calligraphic Trace

> Effectively, reading the Qur'an is meant to inspire trepidation because it directs us to think about death and what follows; it must not be used as a source of pleasure for people looking for pleasant sounds.
>
> Ibn Khaldun

> How charming it is that there are words and tones; are not words and tones rainbows and seeming bridges 'twixt the eternally separated?
>
> Friedrich Nietzsche

1. The Fissure of the Sign

A sovereign form of writing, calligraphy denounces, subverts, and reverses the very substance of language while transporting it to an *other-space*, one whose arrangements subject language to an overdetermined variation. It is this movement, vacillating between sound and the written mark, that we investigate here. Like Chinese calligraphy, Arabic calligraphy is an unprecedented form of the sign and a rhetoric of oversignification. A rhetoric? Usually this word is reserved for literary acts. But in this usage there is a strange deviation: Western knowledge originates and fixes meaning within the confines of the spoken word, credited with the double virtue of being the reservoir of meaning and of coming before the written mark. The written mark, by consequence, is obscured, made distant in a secondary function, a function of transvestism.[1] We wish to investigate the following premise, so often forgotten and repressed: Calligraphic writing is a system of tropes that doubles spoken language by a process of ordered oversignification. It is a system that puts language into intersemiotic dialogue.

First, we must distinguish between two facets of Arabic rhetoric: *al-bayân* is not simply the use of figurative language ("beauty marks," says Ibn Khaldun[2]) to organize discourse; it is, generally, the art of precise and elegant exposition, that is, a general rhetoric that applies equally to speaking and writing. "Writing and speaking share the virtue of bayân," al-Qalqashandi writes.[3] Just as the spoken word must be eloquent in order to convince, so must the calligraphic trace be elegant in order to insert itself into the semantic process and open this process to oversignification.

Without the refined rigor of the calligraphic trace, the text is disfigured, as is the process of reading. "The *qalam* [pen] is one of two tongues," as Arabic linguists have said. The expression must be understood in both senses of the word *tongue*. But the image itself troubles and betrays: it can either point to a material knowledge of the sign or serve as the basis for a theological and bureaucratic order, as in the example of celestial bureaucracies. As the double of the tongue and as "the tongue of the hand," the qalam records and fixes the word of God. By the qalam, history is transmitted, that is to say, justified by the reproduction of the metaphysical trace. Al-Qalqashandi, a celestial scribe, maintains the ambivalence of the question: "What is the spoken word?" he asks in a dialogue. "It's the wind passing." "And who can tame it?" "Writing."[4] Thus, the dialectic of speech and writing, especially for Islamic metaphysics, plays with a mode and a theory of the sign that is very specific: Allah is the Creator, who transmits to prophets messages that are carried through—and woven into—their breath. Their bodies are danced in a parabolic movement to the rhythm of rhymed prose.

The originating sign is revealed to Muhammad in a strange vanishing: the divine word is whispered into the transfigured body. This evanescent body, made radiant in a flash, in the blink of an eye, is transported outside time. Divine rhetoric and eloquence are this sealed presence, tattooed—in writing—onto an evanescent body. Tradition tells us that this experience is known to ordinary people only in dreams: only a dream has the quality of being suffused and produced by angelic writing, justifying Freud's contention. Muhammad said, "I have been given words which are concise but comprehensive in meaning."[5] This is, of course, the goal of all rhetoric, but here it is tied to a writing system subject to dissolution. In fact, God treats the universe like a palimpsest. The Qur'an states this very clearly: "God erases or confirms whatever He will, and the source of Scripture is with Him."[6] The human body is a movement of four phases: God kills,[7] gives life, kills, and finally gives life in the beyond, deep in the double book of judgment—paradise and hell.

All of Islamic tradition insists on the Qur'an's revelation as being one of the greatest miracles (*i'jâz*): in the verb *'ajaza*, there is the idea of shattering powerlessness. Rhetoric is thus the product of a miracle whose deciphering imposes on humankind the process of oversignification. Such are, for example, the mysterious isolated letters (*fawâtiḥ*) that begin certain suras of the Qur'an—arbitrary letters outstripping the norms of linguistic economy.

What utterance do these signs that decorate the Qur'an hide in their scattered, glittering appearance? Theologians can conclude without contradicting themselves that "the letters in question were revealed so as to carry the challenge to its paroxysm and to show all Arabs the incapacity of men to produce a comparable book."[8] One of the secrets of the Qur'an is that it transformed letters understood as pure signs into an oversignifying rhetorical argument and that it split the sign from its message, from its utterance, so that in the ear of the believer meaning remains eternally suspended, distant, and shifting. "I will have my sign raised up from the horizon," Muhammad said. The message of the Qur'an is linked to this metamorphosis of language into an enigmatic distraction, a divine game by which the prophets reinvent language. As Massignon says about these isolated letters, "Visions of the Prophet, first in luminous, sonorous touches, isolated consonants at the head of certain suras, before he makes clear how to coordinate them in words, then in sentences."[9] Countering this mystical experience, the disguising of the linguistic sign and its transport bring into being a double writing: a divine writing, the inimitable model of rhetoric; and a worldly writing, which is secondary, derived from the first (in the sense of "drifting away"), and whose function is to make the model into an idol, to fetishize it, and to attempt to depict its miraculous movement. This movement is accomplished by calligraphy with its extreme rigor, which extends to the pure sign in a process that requires a mystical, fetishizing asceticism.[10] The qalam is like the soul of the spoken word—a geometric soul, Plato would have said. It must decipher and transcribe the inimitable spoken word, and it will be repeated in the calligraphy up to the blind spot of gyratory movement: death, the veil put back in place, the void wiped out by the hand of God.

To capture this mystical dimension of the sign, let us turn for a moment to the foundational myth of the origin of Arabic writing. All revelation, the Qur'an teaches, is signed and recorded in an explicit writing. The divine power of such a revelation is graduated and centered on the miracle of the Qur'an. The Qur'an transcends all previous texts; it establishes and governs their hierarchy. What is the source of this power? The mythic system responds by returning to the origin of writing. Here are four versions of this response:

1. Adam wrote words and books three centuries before his death, and after the flood every people discovered his book.
2. Allah reveals writing to Adam in twenty-one tablets.
3. According to Muhammad, every people of belief has a book and the book of Adam corresponds exactly to the Arabic alphabet.
4. The twenty-eight Arabic letters are the divine incarnation in the human body.

If God is the inventor of the Arabic alphabet, then, how are we to distinguish between sacred alphabets and worldly ones? What is the status of difference between languages? Arabic linguists use two distinctions: a mythic distinction (only the alphabets of revealed texts have the mark of the divine hand) and a logical distinction (based upon the arbitrary relation between the phoneme and the written mark). Arab scholars clearly grasped the principle underlying this relation: "In general," says al-Qalqashandi, "there is no established relation between meaning and the sounds of speech, nor between phonemes and written marks. From this source the diversity of languages springs."[11] Jacques Derrida was able to rigorously analyze how the theory of the sign, founded upon the principle of arbitrariness, is linked to the metaphysics of absence and presence. It goes without saying that this hypothesis must be verified and examined in different cultural contexts. The Platonic tradition reduces the written mark to a function of transvestism because the truth of that sign, the spoken word, is the origin of meaning. In Arab learning, the sign is split, rent, in a different way. "Writing," al-Qalqashandi says, "is more useful than speech because the latter conveys only the present, while the former conveys both presence and absence." The Platonic sign is reversed, though the argument still remains within the closure of metaphysics. Writing and speech thus share the force of bayân. The process of signification is the very same as that of the sign in its entirety; it is a process of unveiling, which Arab authors explain so well: "Eloquence [bayân] consists of everything that unveils a hidden meaning, making it fully understood and accepted by the mind."[12] "Bayân," says al-Jahiz, "is the general name of everything that helps you unveil meaning."[13] For al-Jahiz, the theory of bayân, centered on the concept of unveiling, puts signs into five categories: speech; writing; gestures "with the hand, the head, the eyes, the eyebrows and the shoulders [or] with clothing and the sword when the interlocutors are at a distance"; *al-uqud*, the act of counting without speaking or writing, that is to say, with the fingers and their joints; *an-nisbâ*, the spoken word of the earth, of the heavens, and of the wind, for example, or the mystical notion that inspires the astrological theories of Arabic writing and that makes this alphabet correspond to the lunar cycle.[14] Similarly for the act of writing from right to left or from left to right: in the first case, the hand follows the movement of the stars that move from East to West; and in the second case, the hand follows the movement of the seven stars that move backward.

Where can this logico-mystical hierarchy lead us, if not to the splitting of the sign? Without writing, Ibn Khaldun says, the spoken word is dead. At the same time, the universal semiotics that makes the stars speak imposes on humans the process of a terrorizing spoken word—this exterior and vertiginous voice that holds the secret of meaning suspended twice over, in the voice of God and in the arbitrariness of the sign. Ceaselessly, the divine voice suffuses the body and the visions of humans: what I communicate to my interlocutor is not so much the trace of this voice as the system of the articulation of phonemes. God is the creator of alphabets and compound words, and humans are the artisans of their combinations, situated only at the level of the second articulation. Now it is necessary to cite Ibn Khaldun at length:

> Discourse is formed from compound words that God created in the organ of the tongue, with phonetic combinations produced by the uvula and the tongue, so that humans can communicate their thoughts through language. That is the first step of written communication (*kitâba*).
>
> Writing transforms letters as written marks into the verbal expressions of the imagination, and the latter into the ideas found in the soul. The person who writes thus proceeds without stop from one symbol (*dalîl*) to another. . . . Their spirit, led along in this work, passes from the container to that which it contains: this is the intellectual speculation that allows the expansion of knowledge. The ceaseless repetition of going from the signifier to the signified finishes by producing the habit of discernment (*ta'qîl*).[15]

A possible reading of this quotation is that the articulation of signs is regulated in the last instance by writing, which is the center inscribed in God's word; from there to signification ("the thinking of the soul"), writing assures an economy of rupture and continuity or, if you prefer, of overdetermined articulation. Similarly, the process of the sign vacillates between writing as the productive truth of meaning and oblique writing as given breath by a voice external to language, an oblique writing impregnated by an already accredited meaning. Between essence and appearance, writing traces the sign's fissure and the memory of such a movement. It is in the interstices of two forms of writing that Arabic calligraphy compounds the boundless gesture of repetition.

The fissure of the sign, a double writing, a disguising of the divine voice: the setting of calligraphy supplies a transitory, limited fiction that idolizes repetition to the point of exploding the order of language and of giving life to the artifice of the gesture and of vision.

2. Polygraphy

Placed within a general semiotics, calligraphy is, without a doubt, an exalted and mobile rhetoric whose abundance of figures transforms language into a meditative posture. It links and exceeds language with a tripartite register: phonetic, semantic, and geometric. The phoneme of course forms the basis of calligraphy's laws and its readability, but the calligraphic trace tears and repairs it in a more musical manner. The phoneme is thus the sign of the birth of polyphony. The calligraphic trace makes possible a reading of multiple dimensions, located each time in the interstice of a circular movement, and it introduces into the linguistic system the sound of a suspended music. The semantic level is no less exciting: the oversignification developed in this process annuls the usual meaning that the énoncé produces. In this, there is a sensual pleasure that calligraphic knowledge dramatizes and that is the source of its extreme ambivalence: pleasure, in working against the conventional origin of meaning, creates as an externalized object the substance from which it emerges. And it is precisely the rhetoric of calligraphy, organized principally by geometry, that creates a game of postures. The variety of figures and their delicate bravado correct in some way the restrictions binding language. Through its infinite formulas, calligraphy points to the confinement of meaning and disseminates it through a power replete with jouissance, as if in the movement back and forth across these three levels, the mark, the gesture, and musicality compose, by an expansion of language, a moving arrangement.

What is the semiotic status of such a movement? With his habitual rigor (a rigor of jouissance), Lévi-Strauss shows us an approach related to music and Chinese calligraphy:

> Like the latter—but because it is a sort of secondary form of painting—music refers back to a primary level of articulation created by culture: in the one instance, there is a system of ideograms; in the other, a system of musical sounds. But by the mere fact of its creation, the pattern makes explicit certain natural properties: for instance, graphic symbols, particularly those of Chinese writing, display aesthetic properties independent of the intellectual meanings they are intended to convey; and it is these properties that calligraphic art exploits.[16]

If we consider the double articulation no longer as a dogma but as a simple postulate of an overt strategy, we are led, it seems to me, to an even more radical perspective. It is a radicalization suggested by Igor Stravinsky, who enigmatically stated, "Music is first calligraphy." This is a semiotic reversal of which we cannot measure the full significance (which is conceivably immense) but which provides the necessary jouissance for our text: the subtle emotion that sings out from the pleasure of writing and that dissolves delicately into the pure sign by the back-and-forth motion; the effacement of rhetorical abundance; the taking flight, in return, of the intense dazzling or the violent perfume of a look that is itself calligraphic. The point of an argument, the point of a nib. Then begin again.

Articulated twice, music plays on the artifice of its own unique arrangement: music is capable of implementing (by an internal form of critique) and subverting the codes upon which it is based, whereas calligraphy inscribes its originality and its difference in the existence of a third code, which is this dazzling rhetoric that makes language an externalized object while at the same time inserting it into its own arrangements. It goes without saying that the third code semantically signifies only from within language, through relation to the two other levels. There is thus an interruption and a displacement of the process; this is sensible work of visual rhetoric.

The gesture of Arabic calligraphy respects this order. It composes each letter separately, ties them together, then gives voice to them, finally embellishing the entire énoncé—three moments whose vibratory transposition will have to be discussed later and in relation to the three aforementioned levels, namely, the phonetic, the semantic, and the geometric. But first, the Jakobsonian problematic—remarkable in itself—must be dealt with: "the analogy between the role of grammar in poetry and the role of composition in painting";[17] as must Massignon's love for analogies. While discussing Arab arts, Massignon writes, "Triple vocalization is thus the basis of Arabic grammar: the *i'râb*. And it is the basis of Semitic musical semantics." A little further on, he writes,

> The triple vocalization is the basis of Semitic musical semantics. The relation of rhythm (that weakens its units) to melody (that attains the soul) is the same as the relation of the consonant-based theme (that provides the formula for the idea) to the vocalization of final sounds (that makes the phrase comprehensible).[18]

Calligraphic writing is no longer of a strictly linguistic order; it is the resonance of its phonetic-semantic geometry. Language precedes it, but the calligraphic trace peels back the veil of its order. The analogy between Arab arts and language is no longer valid. Arab music is principally homophonic, melodic, and vocal; it is based on the interval of the fourth. The temporality of the calligraphic trace is polyphonic, intertextual, and intersemiotic. It is through the help of new musical languages that one day it will be possible to analyze the relation between calligraphy and music. Polyphony? It's more accurate to speak of *polygraphy*. What sings out here, what makes calligraphy exceed language, is this subtle and powerful nonlinguistic combination that suffuses language, disfigures it, and announces a flamboyant celebration of the sign. The visible surface is of course language, but the voyage and the reading necessary for such a migration of vision sets a fiction (of meaning) in play in nothing less than a story saturated with rhetoric, a logical and spatiotemporal rhetoric nonetheless tamed by an integral graphic dimension. In Arabic calligraphy, the triple vocalization explicitly maintains the circular signification in the consonant-based body; the horizontal line on which the text is stationed tends to dissolve and join the oblique and the vertical, or to dissolve into a labyrinthine space of suggestion and drunken analogy. There are so many figures unknitting language in some way, liberating the confounding enigma of desire, the truth beyond the present.

3. Ibn al-Bawwab's Ode to Calligraphy

You who want to excel in calligraphy,
You must devote yourself to your God and Master.
You should prepare a straight and strong reed,
Then, to trim it, choose its narrowest end.
The qalam shouldn't be too long or too short, split it
In the middle, equidistant from each end.
Carving its nib is a secret,
All I can tell you is that it's
All about its form: neither oblique nor round.
As for ink, you will need a deep inkwell,
Where vinegar, verjuice, camphor, soot, and orpiment
Mixed with red ochre produce a fermented paste.
Flatten a white and smooth piece of paper under the press
To clean it and remove creases. Then, slowly,
And patiently, wipe down a wooden slate
And try out some characters.
It will become easier and easier
And your reed will become increasingly docile.
God be praised! What you do now will be read back
To you from the Register of the Day of Resurrection![19]

4. Writing Typologies

We know that the Arabic script—developed from Nabataean Aramaic—is written in principle on a medial line, which is brought into relief by the ascending and descending vertical lines of certain characters and by signs (diacritical vowels and dots). As a whole, the Arabic script gives the impression of a linked cursive, but in fact, it has given life to many extremely different styles, including several that even negate the value of scripts.

As Erwin Panofsky has noted, Arab theories of proportion—like those in Byzantine art—are based on a modular system.[20] (Chinese calligraphers measure letters in quadrants.) This modular system uses a square (sometimes round) dot as its rubric, which serves to measure characters and the blank space around them simultaneously. For the Brothers of Purity, an important ninth- and tenth-century sect, this modular theory was part of a harmonic theory of cosmological and musical inspiration. Many treatises—that of Ibn Muqla, in particular—rigorously define the proportions of calligraphy. It would be interesting to compare the details of all the different styles of Arab art according to its theory of proportion and the corresponding theories in calligraphy, architecture, mosaics, and music. (We will return to this later.)

Following Dominique Sourdel, we reject the opposition said to define Kufic and Naskhi scripts.[21] An opposition exists, by contrast, between Hijazi and Iraqi scripts: at least, that's the belief of Arabic writers and of paleographic scholarship. In our analysis, four principal orientations exist in Arabic scripts (see figure 4.1):

- Angled script: From Old Kufic, which is well adapted for architecture and mosaics. Without a doubt, the most elaborate geometric script.
- Accented cursive script: Farsi, Taʿlīq, and Ruqʿah.
- Folded cursive: Diwani and Tughra. Styles destined for royal seals. Intentionally very complex to prevent all forms of imitation.
- Script with what Massignon calls "open linear projection":[22] Thuluth, Naskhi (which is the most common style), and Andalusian-Maghrebi.

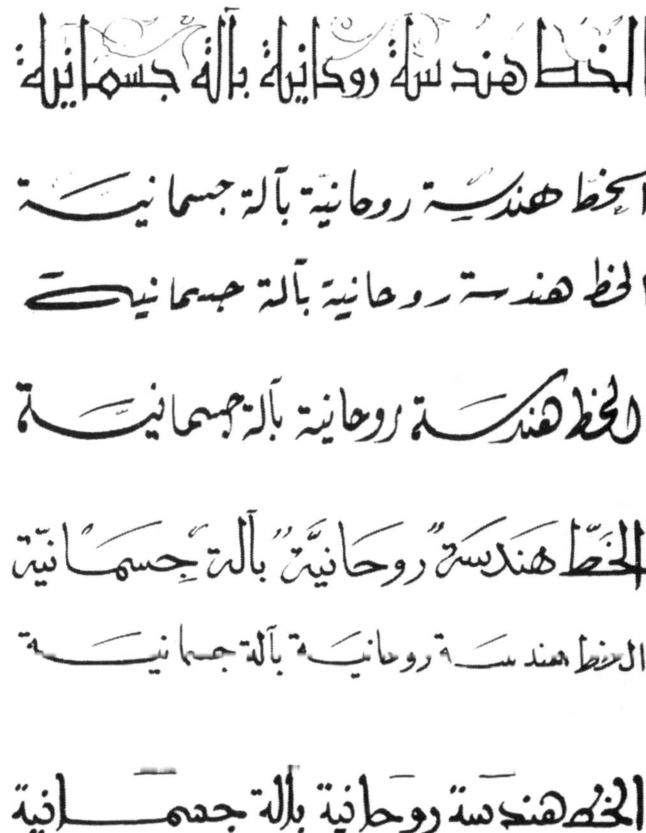

Figure 4.1. Simplified Typology of Arabic Writing Styles, by Muhammed Lemaalmine. The phrase "The geometric writing of the soul articulated by the body" in seven styles: Kufic, Farsi, Diwani, Thuluth, Naskhi, and Andalusian-Maghrebi.

5. Figures

Having quickly laid out this simplified typology, we will now present a few examples. Our work owes much to the Iraqi Naji Zain al-Din's wonderful *Atlas of Arab Calligraphy*.[23] Passionate about Arabic calligraphy, he has dedicated forty years to its study.

Although enjoyable, calligraphy would be pointless if, above and beyond the exquisite leisure of the voyage and the pleasure that it produces, it didn't have an ontological value: a delicate veiling that makes knowledge evanescent and the notion so commonly called beauty fade away. If there is a beauty of the written mark, it must be analyzed from within this intimate relation between the trope and the transformative, enthralling combinatorics of the alphabetic letter.

Figure 4.2. Kufic Calligram Labyrinth.

In the Kufic labyrinth (see figure 4.2), there's a divine deliriousness. The Qur'anic sentence is the text's horizon and affords it transcendental meaning. But the énoncé, whether doxological or not, is put into play by a third code that establishes the burning evasion of vision and the letter, the two mixed together in violent interrogation. This is the aerial and musical disguise of being into and out of the letter that is at stake in the celebrated allegory of the labyrinth. What's a labyrinth? For our example, we're going to use the image described by Roger Caillois, in which

> the itinerary is interminable and labyrinthine, but obligatory. Hesitation is impossible. At any moment, a single corridor is all there is, although constantly curved to the point of giving the impression to anyone in its midst that there's no option of returning in the direction from which you've come. The reality is that you successively have to touch each and every point of the exposed surface.[24]

This is exactly the itinerary proposed here. The sentence begins with the word *Allah* in the bottom corner; it continues in a gyratory movement—sometimes squared, sometimes zigzagging—and ends in the center with the word *al-ʿazʾîm* (the great). This gyration is broken up by readerly interruptions: jumps from one line to another, mirror images and other mirrorlike effects, and many figurative devices—very close to music—that give the reader the power of jouissance. The labyrinth is written out in the scattering of the stars of being. It's a form of writing that self-destructs.

A supreme ruse: except for several identifiable signs, the diacritical dots are actually inside the letters and white (diacritical dots—like vowels—are usually above and below the median line).

The Arabophone reader will enjoy reading the labyrinthine calligram, beginning with the flesh (*al-kursi*) verse of the sura "The Cow" (*al-baqara*). Here's the translation of what is written in the labyrinth's walls:

> Allah! There is no god worthy of worship except Him, the Ever-Living, All-Sustaining. Neither drowsiness nor sleep overtakes Him. To Him belongs whatever is in the heavens and whatever is on the earth. Who could possibly intercede with Him without His permission? He fully knows what is ahead of them and what is behind them, but no one can grasp any of His knowledge—except what He wills to reveal. His Seat encompasses the heavens and the earth, and the preservation of both does not tire Him. For He is the Most High, the Greatest.[25]

The calligraphic labyrinth then ends with the habitual phrase "sadaqa allâh al-ʿazʾîm" (Allah the Almighty speaks the truth) in such a way that the word *ʿazʾîm*, which is written just once in the center of the labyrinth, simultaneously ends the chosen verse and the supplementary phrase. The énoncé can be articulated, regarding the word *ʿazʾîm*, on three levels:

	——	Allah at the beginning of the verse
ʿazʾîm	——	end of the verse
	——	end of the supplementary phrase

Without a doubt the reading principle here is defined by relation to religious finality. But whether the énoncé is religious or not, the calligraphic gesture doubles the énoncé in a spatiotemporal and polygraphic movement that invests it with the power of the combinatorics that already surpasses language, and a simple inversion or a modest phonetic jump will make the word and its signification fall. There is, then, a profound fissure of the sign and the dance of the letter undergoing transfiguration. This is why we said that calligraphy performs a stupefying rhetoric. Little by little, the notion of phonetic-semantic-geometric aftereffects must be materially grasped.

In figure 4.3, reading the Mamluk Kufic calligraphy is easy: the double circle (or the triple circle, so frequent in Byzantine art) symbolizes power. In the outer circle, we can read, "The king rules upon three pillars: compassion, justice, and generosity."

In the inner circle is the name Muhammad Ali. This is the name of the Egyptian king that had the seal made.

Figure 4.3. Mamluk Kufic Calligram.

The frequent utilization in Arabic calligraphy of small decorative signs is important to notice. These are signs that at times have a purely aleatoric graphic function, but that, in other cases, are readable. They are miniature doubles of letters.

Yet the transparency of an énoncé like this is misleading: the centrifugal movement of the *alif* and *lâm* assures the calligraphy of a particular violence: the wound of the name. Our recent (personal and national) history is written between power and the letter. If this wound translates a present day that is too blinding, it also masks the difficulty—the immense difficulty—of conceptualizing history. Because it opens the text to another text, the title of our book has a historical raison d'être.[26]

The inverted writing of figure 4.4—almost entirely legible—derives from a prayer.[27] Here, the Thuluth calligraphy by Hafiz Usman (1642–1698) occupies thirteen lines: six are right side up, and seven are upside down. The énoncés of six pairs of lines are the same in each direction: they are doubles. The line at the top of the figure, the artist's signature, is unreadable right side up; you must traverse the énoncé in both directions before you can finally arrive at it, which thus inaugurates and closes the text. It's a delicate inversion: it makes the énoncé pivot, not just around itself but also toward the inverted center of the person who traced it out. It's the august volume of the name, the principle of essential meaning.

Figure 4.4. Thuluth Calligram.

Otherwise, what's remarkable about this example is the expenditure of the asymmetrical gesture, despite the fact that, at first, we're attuned to its apparent symmetry. The asymmetry is evident on various levels: there are oblique, confident lines; there's a graphic gap between the first and second lines that are right side up; and there's a graphic difference between several characters when comparing the lines with their inversions. It's as though Hafiz Usman was looking to disrupt our knowledge about calligraphy, which is based on symmetry, order, and prudish violence. Asymmetry is no longer the opposite or the (recalcitrant) double of symmetry; it's rigorous movement that pulls the énoncé and the calligraphic trace toward comprehension's vertiginous end and the death of writing.

The calligraphic writing in figure 4.5, in Thuluth and Kufic and by Muhammad Shafiq (1819–1879), creates a mirror.

Figure 4.5. Calligram in Thuluth and Kufic.

> First énoncé (at the top): "The only ones who should tend God's places of worship are those who believe in God."[28]
> Second énoncé (in large letters): "Bismillah."
> Third énoncé (on either side, in Kufic): "I have faith in him."
> Fourth énoncé (in the center, in Kufic): "God Almighty speaks the truth."

The first statement is readable from right to left, and then it's readable in its mirrored image from left to right. The second statement must be read in the following manner: the bismillah legible on the right extends across the entire width, and the bismillah that reflects back cuts across the image from left to right. We don't recommend that the reader enter into this push and pull of mirror reflections: when you look into a mirror, whether you enter into it, or it into you, the result is the same. To make the letter and its double, its body and the image of its body, coincide is doubtlessly an intrusion that speaks of madness and death (see Mallarmé's *Igitur*). This example makes delirium revolve in mirrors, and it makes the veil separating appearance and its reference tremble. So, then, one figure among others of our famous phonetic-semantic-geometric aftereffects becomes visible in a gyratory gesture. Therein also lies a fable-like thought of the sign and its wound (our artificial name), which is divined, spun into disarray, and scattered into vibratory reflection.

We don't think we're dreaming.

A bit of this style tells of an insolent death, which we can ignore or which we can desire. All aestheticism is absent here, even that of lethal beauty.

And, doubtlessly, this supreme vibration will have to articulate in our vision and our body a certain art of living *this*, or *this-now*—this *according-to-which*.

The calligraphic writing in figure 4.6, also in Kufic and Thuluth and also by Muhammad Shafiq, displays coordination. (In fact, this figure contains a third type of writing, called Thuluth Gilli, which we're going to describe below.)

Figure 4.6. Calligram in Thuluth and Kufic.

Here, the Qur'anic words are entirely legible, though this readability, according to the calligraphic law, is only a byway, a pretext for calligraphy.

What's admirable in this case is the exact coordination of the two types of writing (Kufic and Thuluth), a coordination doubled by the explosive movement of the coordinating conjunction *wâw*. We can read the different statements in whatever order we choose, but I recommend beginning with the Kufic throughline, which is the image's focal point. This line begins with the bismillah invocation on top: "In the name of God, the Lord of Mercy, the Giver of Mercy!"[29] Then the calligraphy continues with a statement introduced by the biggest *wâw*—the Lord of *wâw*s, no doubt. From there, the Qur'anic saying is meted out piecemeal, each phrase introduced by another *wâw*, until the *lakinna* brings it back up to the center-left: "But power belongs to God, to his Messenger, and to the believers, though the hypocrites do not know this."[30] Next, we have to read the énoncé written in Thuluth that is above and to the left, "Allah the Almighty speaks the truth." Finally, the seal can be seen in the center of the calligram.

There are languages that use *and* liberally and well. Arabic, which uses it with abandon, transforms the word into a veritable psalm-like refrain. What speaks to the eye and to the ear in this example is the repetition and the under-song, which Louis Massignon liked to speak about. The linguistic sign is made dynamic by the writing. In Ibn Sina's theory of the symbolism of letters, the *wâw* is an uncontrollable letter, which justifies the imperial gesture of this example.[31]

The Tughra monogram in figure 4.7 represents the imprisoning of the name.

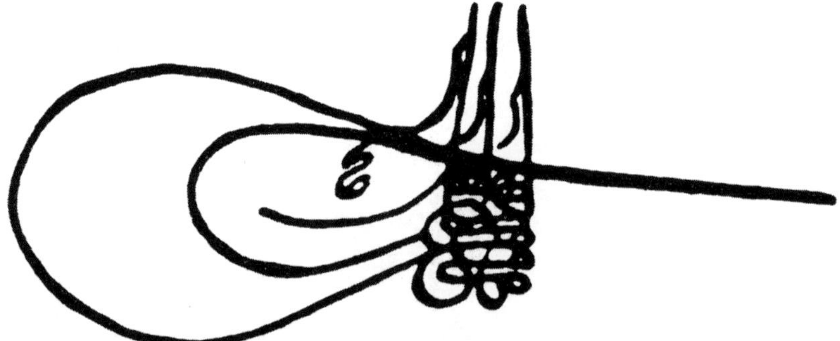

Figure 4.7. Tughra Writing.

This monogram is almost unreadable. A type of ideogram, it embodies unreadability. Nevertheless, we imagine it's the name of Mehmed the Conqueror (1432–1481). In order to escape being an imitation of anything, the symbol of power must be disfigured and, at the same time, introduce a secret language. The visual effacement of the name, the sheer expressivity of initials—this is what denounces the illusion of power, that is to say, the foolish certainty of a center. Power does not have a center.

Arab (and Chinese) art developed from the letter to figural representation, which we know is little tolerated by Islam. Figure 4.8 is a face in words, a clear transgression of the taboo, accentuated by the arbitrary evasion of letters and their organization. The énoncé seems to include four names, but we can't be certain: Allah, Muhammad, ʿAli, and Hussayn or Hasan (ʿAli's sons).

Figure 4.8. A Face in Words.

The right cheek bears the name Hussayn (or Hasan), which is then reflected onto the left cheek (from the reader's perspective). Similarly, the name Muhammad, which begins at the pupil of the right eye, is reflected onto the pupil of the left eye. The name Allah is upside down at the top of the skull, and the name ʿAli—also upside down, though more subtly—starts at the right eyeball, joins the nose, then rapidly folds into the eyebrow. The name ʿAli is also seen in a reflection on the left side when you look at the face upside down.

This rigorous symmetry is based on the two tropes of the mirror and the reversal. Such simplicity is enough to afford the calligraphic trace an astonishing ability to startle the reader: a cadaver-like form becomes a true rhetorical form, a decorative death productive of meaning. Amen!

Chapter 5

The Storyteller's Voice

Recorded on a cassette tape, the peasant voice that retells the story "The Talking Bird" (see the text below) invokes, through a faint nostalgia, the force of a generative movement. It's a voice in which emotions, irony, and even tragedy can be heard but still a voice that knows that storytelling generates its power only from infinite transparency and the mirage of a vibratory music, always reassuring and maternal—a maternity that is in some ways torn, since it is only through the orphaned circulation of the name that it exists, will ever exist, and will ever grant to the story the object of its voyage. The story is enveloped by music, based in music through a plucked effraction, and tied to the disposition of a voice that seems evaporated in myth while, at the same time, repeating the same psalm-like refrain about our ruined innocence. And, no doubt, we no longer know how to listen to the story; it does not have the formal dimension that fascinates the contemporary mind. But, in its vocal intensity, it evokes the cry, the shout, which comes from somewhere—even if no one knows exactly where. In the end, what would such a genealogy matter? What we hear now is this voice that establishes the meaning of the tale and its genealogy. Theoretical reversal is necessary here so that the voyage stitched together can activate our memory with the one phrase that always forces us to listen: "once upon a time." Repetition is a joyful power, an evanescent particle of our being, floating freely in the generative and gyratory movement that seizes us. The rarity and the luxury of the orphan voyage is the path staked out in this scene from Scheherazade.

What this voice tells us is, for our current state of knowledge, something strangely forgotten. We have forgotten that the story belongs to the order of the voice and music; and, more exactly, it is, in relation to the voice, a particular arrangement of its trace. It's the voice heard in its most materialistic movement (with no relation to the voice of the metaphysical sign), combining its language in an intonation and a composition that, though they are reducible to language, are an execution brought—stolen—from the linguistic code.

Claude Lévi-Strauss speaks of an illustrative incident in his life. It is well known that after seeing barbarity in others he admitted the same in himself. He took a day in the field to meditate on the orphanhood that made him wander across an ineffable difference, and he felt himself soften while listening to an internal voice that brusquely assailed him. A motif from Chopin grew there, although he was Wagnerian. Why was he beset by this nostalgia? this voice? In a fit of nostalgia, the wound of the name announces and inscribes in Lévi-Strauss the quality of a delight linking the voice to storytelling. Where does Lévi-Strauss draw (for our aurality) his incomparable power, even delirium (methodological or not), if not in the dissolving gyration that shatters the illusion of transparent identity and difference? We should be grateful to him for having reopened the question of storytelling by telling his own story. Or, stated more exactly, storytelling is a voice, a combinatorics granting people a power of jouissance against the forces of entropy. The story is like music but *like* in an open-ended sense that we want to interrogate here, after giving the translation of "The Talking Bird," a translation that owes much to A. Diouri.

Here's the tale.

"THE TALKING BIRD"

Once upon a time, there was a sultan who, although married, didn't have children. A tribe gave him the gift of a young woman whom he could take as a wife. She became pregnant.

Just when that wife was soon to give birth, the sultan had to leave for war. He asked others to look after her. But his other wives instead got ready to play a nasty trick on her. They brought home a puppy, bribed the midwife, and on the day of the birth, took the child for themselves and set the puppy in its place. When the poor woman sat up, she saw that she was surrounded. She heard them say, "The sultan's wife has given birth to a puppy!"

As for the baby, the other wives hid it in a chest with a little money. Then, they wrapped it up and gave it to a woman, saying, "Take it and kill it." The woman replied, "No, I'll throw it into the sea." She did, then returned home.

One day, a fisherman in another country found the chest and took it home. He opened it and saw the baby. Just like the sultan, the fisherman didn't have any kids. He said, "Thanks be to Allah for bringing me this gift!" He brought up the child and planted a fig tree in his honor.

When the sultan returned home from the war, they said to him, "Welcome home, Sultan! Your child is in the foyer. . . . Your wife has given birth to a puppy." And he said, "Thanks be to Allah for granting me my wish, even if it is a puppy. Praise be to Allah!" Nothing changed. The young wife—that poor woman—was trapped. She avoided the puppy and didn't do anything to care for it. Now as before, she got pregnant—thanks be to Allah. Again, she gave birth to a boy. And again, the sultan's other wives used the same trick, exchanging the prince for a puppy. All told, the poor woman was the victim of that same treachery three times: two boys and a girl were taken from her and recovered by the same fisherman. For each, the fisherman planted a fig tree.

The children grew up. The fisherman took good care of them. The sultan rejected his unfortunate wife. "Enough of this," he said. "I'm not a dog that I should bear puppies. I have to have . . . I'm a sultan! . . . a human! I'm not going to put up with people congratulating me for having dogs! Enough's enough! May Allah forgive me!"

The poor wife! What could she do? She was sent to live with the servants and slaves. No one cared one way or another.

So, the fisherman's kids grew up. They became strapping youths. They were adept at horse riding. They were so accomplished; none could compare. They were incomparable in knowledge and in every other thing. The fisherman had taught them so well. The girl was no different. They were amazing at everything they did.

The boys participated in riding events and festivals organized by the sultan. The sultan began to like them.

The vizier—viziers are enemies of Allah—saw how the sultan reacted to them, and he thought to himself, "I have to do something. . . . The sultan will soon bring them into his fold and give them state functions, and nothing will be left for me. It would be better to make them disappear once and for all."

The vizier told the sultan, "Sir, I have something to say! You'll never be able to accomplish all you want without meeting the talking bird. Your kingship will never be fully respected."

"You don't say!" the sultan replied. "And who will bring it to me? And where is this talking bird found?"

"In a country far away."

"Who will bring it here?"

"If not the fisherman's kids, then no one."

"OK," said the sultan. He called for the fisherman, and the fisherman came—scared witless, the poor guy!

He prostrated before the sultan. "What do you want, Sultan?"

"Nothing important," the sultan replied. "I want your kids to bring me the talking bird. And if they don't, I'll cut off your head and then I'll cut off theirs."

The fisherman returned home. He cried.

"What's wrong, Dad?" one of his sons asked.

The father repeated what the sultan had said. The son said, "I'll go find this talking bird, wherever it is. Don't worry!"

So, the son got together provisions and everything he would need for the trip. He mounted his steed and left. One child—the oldest—gone.

He went on and on and on, through country after country. Only Allah—hallowed be his almighty name!—can turn a country into a desert or breathe life into it. He went on and on and on. He reached the forest of the talking bird. He met a man, who asked him, "Where are you heading, good man—you who don't deserve misfortune?"

"Sir," the child said, "I'm actually looking for misfortune."

"Where, my son?"

"I'm looking for the talking bird."

"God, God! O my son!" the man yelled. "How many men have fallen trying to capture it!"

"What do you mean?" the boy asked.

"After you leave here, my son, and when you reach the talking bird, it will start to tell you the story of your life. It will know your name, and it will tell you so much about your life that you'll grow tired. You'll say, 'Yes, yes!' But the moment you say yes, you'll be swallowed. The ground will swallow you; it will close over you, your horse, your provisions, and all that you own."

"That's it?" the fisherman's son asked.

"Yes."

"Then I won't say yes," the boy proudly said.

"O my son, if Allah has mercy upon you, you won't say yes and you'll be saved. You'll capture the talking bird."

"How?"

"After you leave here, my son, you'll find a boulder on your path. You'll sacrifice a sheep on this boulder. You'll leave the sheep there, and you'll sit further away. Just make sure you don't say yes. If you follow these rules, you'll capture it. But if you say yes, it will be all over for you."

The child left.

The birds flew in. They came alone, in pairs, and in flocks; they kept coming and coming to the point that everything in the world that was a bird and that nested in the night under the wings of the talking bird was there. The talking bird arrived and, being so large, gathered them under its wings. All the birds fell under its shadow. The talking bird started its tale: "Listen, birds, to the history of the night. Once upon a time, there was a sultan. . . . A tribe gave him the gift of a young woman whom he could take as his wife. She became pregnant. The sultan's other wives wished her ill; they bribed the midwife, stole the baby, and replaced it with a puppy. They threw the baby into the sea. A fisherman found it. He raised the child—and two more. They grew up in his home. They participated in the horse-riding festival of the sultan, who looked upon them kindly. The vizier became jealous and called for the fisherman. He ordered him to send his children off to look for the talking bird to entertain the sultan. This bird was called the Bird of birds."

The bird's story was never-ending. Finally, the fisherman's son said, "Yes, yes!" Blessed be our prophet! At that very moment, the young man disappeared. The ground swallowed him up along with his horse and all his belongings. The earth had swallowed him. Walking through his yard that day, the fisherman saw this son's fig tree wither. He ran to his wife, crying, "Woe! Woe! My child is dead!"

"What are you talking about?" his wife asked.

"His life is over," he replied. "The fig tree has withered."

Then his brother said, "I'll go look for him."

"No, stay here," his father said to him.

"No. The river that has taken away my brother will take me away as well. I'm going to join him, no matter what."

Then he gathered his belongings, provisions, and pistol. He left. He met the man his brother had already met. The man said, "Hello, there!"

"Hello to you as well," he replied.

"Where are you going, you who deserve no misfortune?"

"Sir, that's exactly what I'm looking for."

"Where are you going, my son?"

"Sir, I'm looking for the talking bird."

"O God! O my son! How many men have gone looking for it without one ever capturing it! They're all gone for good!"

"But why? What's so special about this bird?"

"My son, they didn't even put up a fight. The bird will only talk to you; it will tell you the story of your life. You'll try to resist, but you'll end up saying yes. Then the ground will swallow you up."

"So I won't say yes, God willing."

"So go and don't say yes."

He left.

He resisted for as long as he could but finally said yes, just like his brother. The bird told him the story of his life. The child spoke, like his brother, and the bird swallowed him.

The next day, the fisherman saw the second fig tree wither and die. He said through his tears, "What can I do, now that both of my sons are dead?"

His daughter said to him, "I'll go join my brothers, and I'll bring back the talking bird." So she gathered her things, just like a man would. She did so without brooking any objection. She gathered her pistol and her food, and she left.

She went on and on, from one country to another. She met the same man her brothers had met. "Hello, there!" she said.

"Hello to you too! May Allah bless you! Where are you going, my dear?"

"Sir, I'm off to capture the talking bird. Is this where it lives?"

"My dear, bearded and valiant men have tried and failed to do what you say you want to do."

"Just tell me where it is," she said, "and Allah will bless your parents. Tell me where to go and how I can avoid misfortune. Then I'll capture the bird, with Allah's help."

The man gave her instructions, saying, "You'll find a boulder where you need to make a sacrifice. You'll approach the bird and listen to it. It will talk only about you, but you must never say a single word."

"Two boys—my brothers—have already come to capture it."

"Those were your brothers?"

"Yes."

"Beware, my girl, beware! When you capture it, make sure you say 'I won't free you until you give me back my brothers.' If it proposes to give them back as slaves, say no; as Black men, say no; or as ogres, say no. Tell it to give them back just as they were when it swallowed them. Just as they were, with their horses, their clothes, their faces. Tell it that only then will you free it. The bird will ask you to perform a sacrifice on the boulder. After the sacrifice, your brothers will emerge from the earth, with their horses, weapons, and everything else. At that moment, you will quickly imprison it in the chest and carry it with you. Don't accept any deformed brothers! They should be just as they were!"

"OK," the girl said. "May Allah bless your parents!"

She left. (You know, we women are patient.) The bird went on talking, telling the story of the girl's life—on and on, until it grew tired. But the girl remained silent. "There's nothing you can do," she told the bird. "You can go on with your story all night long, but I'm not going to talk." She said nothing and just watched. She took her horse to graze and said nothing. Tired, the talking bird fell asleep. Seeing that the bird was in a deep sleep, she opened her chest and threw it inside.

The man of the forest had told her, "Beware, don't let it go! If you let it go, it's curtains for you! Guard it well!" She guarded the bird well, like a blind man clinging to his attendant. She took the chest and started off.

"Let me go, daughter of the sultan!" the bird said. "Let me go!"

"Not until you've given me back my brothers."

"Let me go!" he screamed.

"With Allah as my witness, I won't let you go until you give me back my brothers. I came here for my brothers, whom you've swallowed."

"And if I give them back?"

"Give them back and I'll free you."

"How do you want them? As slaves?"

"No, as my brothers."

"What about ogres, with teeth that jut out?"

"As my brothers. They have to be just as they were when you swallowed them."

"And you'll free me?"

"I'll free you."

"Then go perform a sacrifice on that boulder," the talking bird said. She gathered her courage and dealt a strong blow, and the sacrifice was performed. Her brothers emerged from the ground. They said, "O sister! Why are you here? How did you find us?"

"What happened to your courage and virility?" she yelled at them. "You couldn't even resist? You were so well prepared; you'd brought weapons, crossed so many countries to get to the talking bird. And then the talking bird fooled you!"

"O sister, it was foretold! From the moment we got here, it would not stop telling the stories of our lives. We resisted for as long as we could, until we couldn't take it anymore."

"Oh well," she said. "It's in here now. We're taking it back, by hook or by crook."

The girl and her brothers took the bird and gave it to the sultan, who kept it. The sultan commanded the bird to speak.

"What do you want me to say?" the bird asked him. "Why your kids captured me and brought me here?"

"They're the fisherman's kids," the sultan corrected him.

"They're your kids, not the fisherman's. The fisherman fished them out of the sea and raised them. But they're your kids."

"Then tell me the story of my kids," the sultan said.

"They're the kids you had with the young bride from that tribe. She got pregnant; your other wives got jealous. They bribed the midwife, and when the baby was born, they replaced the child with a puppy, whose eyes were still shut tight like a baby's."

"And afterward?" the sultan asked.

"When people came to congratulate you, you said, 'All praise be to Allah, even if he gave me a puppy. Thanks be to Allah!' The first time, you thanked Allah; the second time too. Then the third time, you got upset. And now, why do you make that poor girl suffer? Your children are hers, and her children are yours."

The vizier was dumbfounded. The sultan went to his wives and the midwife. He tied them on one side to a camel suffering from horrible thirst, and on the other to a camel suffering from horrible hunger; they were drawn and quartered. Then he burned them in a giant pyre.

The kids went home to the sultan who abdicated, ceding power to the fisherman. They were happy, every single person. "So, Vizier," the sultan said, "your tricks have all come home to roost, and in the end, the fisherman and the children have taken advantage of them!"

Told by Lalla Myriem
(fifty years old, illiterate)
Duoar Jdid, near Sidi Slimane,
Morocco
March 12, 1971

Scheherazade's Voice

We too say no to the talking bird, but this mysterious negation deserves to be even further obscured. "To obscure the obscure," states the Tao.[1] This is knowledge's ascetic motif, which dissolves in its own utterance; its "truth" is to tear open confinement, the confinement of meaning. Its rhetoric is blind, universally blind. It measures, in relation to the text, the balance of the most sophisticated postures, without fear of contradictions or delirium. It's all illusory, perhaps, in terms of methodology: what I say about knowledge is a breach into that which is opposed to knowledge *without* text or writing. Like the name, the text is orphaned. This is an assertion that must be further obscured: the night of Scheherazade will be the place of the text's authoritative jouissance. But that's getting ahead of ourselves.

"Half the art of storytelling," writes Walter Benjamin, "[is] to keep a story being told free from explanation as one reproduces it."[2] Indeed, the tale's reasoning comes from within itself (this is also one of Lévi-Strauss's points).[3] It's quite strange to be prevented from thinking on our own! This occurs because of how the narrator's voice, mythic time, and the rhetoric of the pure act—which form the basis of narrative discourse—dissolve repetition's gyratory charm in us, or against us, and reappropriate the transfigured part of the intelligible in the act of listening. There is no end, however, to this dilemma: we must voluntarily confront the illusory delight of our receptivity. A reverie, even when stimulating, is a vexing image; so long as the mirage of the text lasts, the ambiguity that makes the dream attractive to our minds remains the focus of the fantasy's obscure elegance. We end up loving the tale, as a sort of dream, for one more specific reason: to love a fairy tale exactly as it is, and to love it passionately for no reason other than the timbre of the voice, is a striking sign that gives back to the voice its magical power, which will later be negated only under rational analysis, although the quavering of the voice never stops entering into us, speaking to us, and speaking with the critical understanding that permeates it.

What narrative discourse usually lacks are rules governing repetition and closure. Seen from this perspective, the fairy tale is, for formalist analysis, an unparalleled temptation: the taxonomy of narrative functions and their transformation settles the mind's misgivings. Against this temptation, the virtue of the Barthesian text is to have done away with all that; formalist analysis is useful here only as a backdrop, where the shadows put into relief both taxonomical knowledge and its truth. Formalists are like jewelers; jouissance is constrained in settings. But let's leave formalism to its methodological delirium and try to tease out the narrative enigma.

First there is this, which doesn't contradict formalism: the fairy tale is not a delimited entity; it's truly a narrative machine, or if you prefer, a "desiring machine," by which the unconscious enunciates the sovereignty of the pure act for all to hear. What makes the vital violence of the fairy tale the opposite of that of the dream is, incontestably, the unlimited possibility that sings in the narrative voice. This voice teaches us that the hand that holds the die destroys itself in the drunken desire to provoke life and its limits. The fairy tale recounts the impossible, and it produces in our minds a strange satisfaction: the imperial pride of opening life to the pure act. The thinking of the day must be reversed: it's not the body that's a discourse, but the body that's the obscure image of the infinity of orphaned texts. The body is a volatile carving.

The story is a narrative machine of the pure act, which means that the analysis of one *particular* fairy tale will never be privileged over others, even though this might be entirely legitimate and even desirable as an exercise; instead the emphasis will be placed on the generative movement of storytelling. To say yes to the talking bird is to accept the reversal of the narrative logic; the action takes these wily subtleties from formalism. While anti-speculative and anti-psychological, the voice that promises and announces the timbre of the pure act also promises the image of an intense bodily readiness: as has already been suggested, oral literature is based on a violent urge's added value. Later, we'll see the unexpected result of such an economy. The daughter of the king/fisherman utters an unmistakable no, with an irony that amuses all her admirers: "Rhetoric, which puts the lives of my brothers and myself at risk, doesn't interest me," she says to herself. "I understood perfectly well that the fairy tale is a machine built to oppose rhetoric (and this is the source of the timbre of my irony). Or, more exactly, it's a rhetoric of the pure act. What literary critics have called for centuries the 'real' and the 'realistic' presents an illusory opposition. If there were an opposition, it would be between a moral and psychological rhetoric (as in novels) and a rhetoric of the pure act (as in a rolling of the dice)."

Let's set this androgynous and doctored voice aside for a moment, with a second proposition: as a generative movement, the story is an expenditure, a celebration of orality. What does the talking bird say? A multilayered tale. On first reading, it's the well-known tale: the voice repeats the voice; the tale encloses within itself another tale, an infinity of tales. A polyphonic structure with multiple facets articulates an anonymous utterance. Let's go so far as to say that in this case the story is defined as the generative movement slotted between the pure act and nonsense. That repetition occurs due to a damaged nostalgia for an essential meaning is self-evidently part of the narrative metaphysics. But repetition's cyclical formation turns passionate overuse into a gyratory slap that produces meaning. What comforts the formalist mind (when it is satisfied with its tinkering) is exactly the logico-spatial schema, easily applied to the tale's seeming lack of seriousness. As a hollow logical structure, formalism is limited; narrative excess and its anti-rhetorical beauty reject formalism as a rational schema of little value. In other words, storytelling is irrepressible, and the talking bird certainly reproduces a certain theory of speech (speech within speech, etc.). At the same time, the story defines an explicit theory of orality against this tautology. Its transparent style so disturbs us that we can imagine an ironic virtuosity, a certain gesture of consumption, and the insistence of a very pleasing voice that says, "Please excuse my innocence."

Does it mean nothing, then? Here, the subject of utterance, scattered about, has two facets: First, a historical subject, that is, tribal-feudal society. The tribe *gives* a daughter to the king (as was the custom in Morocco). But this is a poisoned gift, the tale comes close to saying. The act of allegiance is transformed through three unlucky rolls of the dice: a puppy, then another puppy, and then a third puppy. After the third, the king no longer thanks Allah; his words to God having become useless, he responds in another unlucky manner. The fairy tale has no scruples about insisting on the infinite misfortune of humankind. The added value of misfortune is one of jouissance's intense powers: the children of the king and the fisherman joyously declare that they are looking for misfortune. The pure act meddles with the theoretical rules of chance, attributing a warlike violence to the initial object (here, the young woman given to the king); its strategy proposes a parapsychological game—the inexorable procedure of a warlike expenditure. It's a war played with dice, to be clear.

The sultan goes off to war, and when he returns, he's told that a dog has been born to him. The poor sultan! The roll of the unlucky dice should push him toward disbelief or madness. His august royalty is reduced to a parodic image: the mystical transmission of blood—which defines the patriarchy—grants him a puppy. The genealogical tree is blocked: the sultan can now only reign over a kingdom of dogs. But that would be another story. How can such a parodic fate be defeated? This is where the tale's journey begins: it is not a simple transfiguration of social relations but a true parody of the historical subject. It is a theme that is concealed, to be sure, behind a moral lesson: at the end of the tale, the sultan abdicates power to the fisherman. Irony upon irony: power is here a narrative excess necessary to the story's ludic function, which consists of replacing one sign with another and so of parodying the violence of social relations. Clearly, a tribal-feudal society is neither its own utterance nor the place of its own illusions. Its utterance plays out in a discourse that is endlessly worked over by the divine voice and yet appears only through gaps and breaks.

The second facet of the historical subject will have to be seen in movement. Story, as communal property, is anonymous (the author, like power, is everywhere) and without a proprietary inscription. What is an author? The censor who controls the circulation of texts and who appropriates for himself the added value of the collective imagination. It's an added value that the censor-author gussies up in the ideology of the solitary creator. Against the stolen signature, then, is exactly where the deep wound of the author's name is to be found.

This added value is linked to a particular context. It's the despotic or bourgeois state that enacts the division in the "empire of signs": next to the official scribe, there's the individual scribe who protects the law as they see fit; the individual scribe constitutes the other pole—a weak one, for sure—of despotic or bourgeois power. The story has the privilege—and it's huge—of decentering the individual appropriation of signs. And because the author's mark is absent here, it's only the text's sovereignty that must be questioned. This does not mean, obviously, that we're calling for a return to artistic tribalism and its violent marks—only that we insist on this political principle:

the text's nonappropriation can establish a power of future revolutionary jouissance.

It's an anonymous literature: the "I" who tells the story is reduced to the voice's timbre and to the thematic variation restructuring the story. Methodologically, we can—as Lévi-Strauss did for his mythic story—inaugurate its analysis and its text by a unity of reference, even if it means drawing the circle tighter and tighter over the narrative tissue's transformation and the invariant quotient's space. We choose—in the analytic trace that we propose—another point of gyratory attack: we work on two versions of "The Talking Bird," the one recounted above and the one from *One Thousand and One Nights*, the first coming from the second. The reader will be able to follow our references through the beautiful translation of Antoine Galland.[4] The story is entitled "The Story of Two Sisters Jealous of Their Younger Sister."[5] Our remarks are made in the in-between between the two stories.

Why are we taking this approach? It's based on a postulate of writing, which tries to seize through an oblique movement the in-between between two stories and to cleave an open inscription, confirming the text's division. It's a principle in keeping with Mallarmé: "Everything takes place, in sections, by supposition; narrative is avoided. In addition this use of the bare thought with its retreats, prolongations, and flights, by reason of its very design, for anyone wishing to read it aloud, results in a score."[6] We're opposing the story's logic and its vocal effervescence to a gyratory, forbidden alterity that is proffered in the power of jouissance. Let's accept this glimpse into duality, and let's see in these different faces the two variants of "The Talking Bird."

The Name

The differences in the story are sometimes small, sometimes enormous. In the second variant, the two brothers and the sister have beautiful names: Bahman, Parviz, and Parizade. For names to be effectively realistic, a certain portrait of identity (and writing) must be possible: as an orphaned sign, the name constrains the text to the thinking of a nomadic identity, expropriated in the desire for the other. "All identity," Pierre Klossowski says, "rests on the knowledge of a thinking agent outside of ourselves—assuming an outside and inside—a thinking person who consents from the outside to think of us as we are."[7] The talking bird allows this expropriation, for example, through the indexes that signal to Parizade the fate of her brothers—one of whom left behind a knife, and the other a rosary. The death of her brothers is indicated in one case by the appearance of a droplet of blood on the knife; in the other, by the immobility of one of the rosary's beads, which blocks each part of the circulatory game of the others. These indexes transfigure incestuous desire; they mark the wound of the name. A "full arabesque," the name brings to life the sign of an unlimited palimpsest. It must be the object (for the analyst) of a special attention. Bahman! Parviz! Parizade! And so on and so forth, up to transfixed knowledge.

The Gift and the Wish

In the first variant, the tribe gives a girl to the sultan, who takes her as his wife. This is essentially a Moroccan custom based on the client system that existed between tribes and the central power. The female narrator substitutes the wish for another cultural index. In *One Thousand and One Nights*, the sultan, in disguise, listens near the front door of his house while the three sisters come up with wishes: the first wants to wed the sultan's baker; the second, the cook; and the youngest, the sultan himself. The pure act suppresses the dream by immediately making it come true; the sultan takes these wishes literally in order to live out his fantasies. The pure and volatile act returns to the relation of social classes: the sultan effectively treats his subjects as his perverted Other. And so, the rupture from the real plays out through the limitless scope of what is possible. It's, a priori, the magical effervescence of gestural movement.

The youngest daughter marries the sultan. That her dream comes true makes the rivalry between her and her sisters explode, and it realizes another fantasy: the death of the Other, the fraternal death of the Other, or the incestuous passion inscribed in the limitless scope of what is possible.

In the second variant, Parizade, the youngest daughter, wants to possess—to complete her fraternal happiness—the three wonders that she lacks, including the talking bird. She sends her brothers to their death. Then she resuscitates them. To wish for something is a chain controlled by crimes against the real. This is where the myth's extreme power comes from: we will see how the chant, music, and miraculous water give birth to this incestuous passion.

The gift allows a political contract; the wish permits a ruling of the pure act. From one to the other, rolls of the die construct the story. From one story to the other, [the art of substitution] the puppy is replaced by a dead puppy and, in the third birth, by a piece of wood. It's too much for His August Majesty! Let's consider it this way: The king of the chessboard slips by chance, pure and simple, into misfortune. Who, then, moves the story's pawns? By a gyratory necessity, the game devolves, implodes; chance is a transfiguration of the pure act. From one king to another, the story makes the barriers of the impossible tumble. And, from one gestural movement to another, the in-between between the two kings is desacralized. An orgy of bad indexes corrupts patriarchal ideology and blood's mythic transmission. From one story to the other, [a mythic cross] what does the tale say in its doubleness? The riddle of the talking bird takes place at the moment of a forbidden yes. To consent at that moment, which is to agree to listen to the story of your life, leads to death's doorstep. The act of listening and death are confused; their end points line up. In organizing the story of woe, the talking bird weaves repetition's gyratory thread around and around. It's true that in an obscure attraction, the forbidden yes situates the actors between life and the death of their name. To say yes, to say the name, is tantamount to accepting, at the moment of its wound, the world's infinite text.

In *One Thousand and One Nights*, there is a more complex version of this myth of the talking bird. To get to the talking bird, the character must meet a dervish, who disappears at the story's end; the narrator wonders how the dervish dies: "It's impossible to know if it was due to old age or if it was because he was no longer needed to lead Princess Parizade to triumph over the three things."[8] (This remark by the narrator passes without anyone commenting on it.) The dervish gives the necessary instructions: don't be scared of the voices of invisible beings and don't turn around. If one does, one gets turned into stone. Like Odysseus, Parizade emerges victorious thanks to a trick: she stuffs her ears full of cotton. She takes home the three wonders: the talking bird, a branch from the singing tree, and a flask of golden water that increases fertility eternally. There is, then, a miraculous added value that risks overshadowing the Orphic myth's power, shown here in a specific figure. It's a power that is so much larger as to be linked to the myth of the sirens. These are the two myths about which Maurice Blanchot wrote so admirably, treating them as representative of the very desire to write.

The transformation of the riddle (to say yes or not) into the Orphic story is radical, although the myth of the talking bird acquires a function close to the siren's song, represented here by the voices of invisible beings who have been turned to stone. A similar function: the rapture of the body by a song of transformation.

The comparison must be made excessive. Dancing. The myth of the talking bird exemplifies a specific theory of oral literature that relies on a magical worldview. This literature, however, includes in it an ontological theory of value that is truly sophisticated; this sophistication must be given its fullest and subtlest value so as to seize "pure rhythmic motifs of being" in the text.[9] We have seen how the figural artifice of tattooing and the calligraphic trace emit effervescent reflections of being by scratching onto the lettered body a delirious rhetoric and a rhythm of dead symbols: language's dynamism, the chant of the fissured being, the name's gyratory wound. So many new limits for meaning and its production. This knowledge creates a never-before-seen intersemiotics. In place of the pure sign, the tale substitutes the pure act. This is exactly what Ernst Bloch proposes: "In fairy tales, thinking takes place only to do, to do only what is right: thinking precedes doing; doing authenticates thinking."[10] This is clearly a metaphysics of the origin and of repetition. But the pure act institutes a veritable repetitive jouissance, including the figure of reversals. In "The Talking Bird," one brother imitates the other and the sister challenges her brothers by ironically erasing the path of their words with an offhand counter-paraleipsis:[11] "I'll say no," she says to the talking bird. The counter-paraleipsis eliminates contradiction; it is, ironically, an indirect and sophisticated way of making the pure act dance.

The tearing apart of repetition, the sovereignty of the pure act—these are the major motifs that decorate this tale's meaning. And they are evident only indirectly.

Let's add another chord to the Orphic zither: "Mounted on the vessel, Orpheus takes his lyre and enchants the sirens to the point that they turn mute and throw their instruments into the sea."[12] The song can be defeated only through a more violent song or, as in Odysseus's example, by a ruse. And what can the sirens hope for but to be dissolved in the song? In the song there's a freshness, a blind force, and a malediction of hope, all of which outline the scope of the possible tear. It's clearly the act of hearing that sees, and in this rapture of the transformed body, we see the interstitial evasion of our destiny parade in front of us—in the heart of the myth. Music allows this prodigious wait in the face of time, bringing about a volatile punctuation of our being, of our being in time.

This division of being is otherwise inscribed in the tale before us. What are Parizade and her brothers looking for? Don't be misled by the luxe promised by the three wonders: the possession of these wonders sends the children back to the paternal cradle. Once possessed, the talking bird is political. It can build and undo kingdoms. This is the gist of the story.

But the incestuous link never offered, never revealed, is inscribed in the life-and-death journey, which gives the riddle its tremendous power. This passion for luxury and this flight toward the unknown—which consume the dreamed-of hymen, split in two—contradict the incestuous desire. "Hymenaeus, Hymen! O Hymen, Hymenaeus!" chanted the Athenians. A transparent motif must be given to this allegory: as the bloody knife slides into Parizade's hand, the rosary beads lock into place. These are, in both instances, the moan of fraternal orgasm, drowned and transfigured into stone. Beyond this cry that stymies the story, everything becomes possible. The cry and the song are the ripping and the delirious law of the incestuous desire. Everything becomes possible, the tale tells us, even happiness. It is, in the end, another roll of the die—a little talkative. And musical, wouldn't you say? Everything becomes possible: the father finds his image again—which isn't something to minimize—and the brothers and sister find the song of their incest. It's as though music, in playing with existence, pushed us toward the scriptural limit of our body by making us see, feel, and taste a truly bizarre passion—that of reducing our right to dream. Music clarifies in its movement the sparkling hieroglyphs of our being and presses the dream into an exclusive language, the guarantor of a disassociated silence and a living death.

Because we make the two ends of the mythic rosary tremble, we think we're able to perceive in this interval a signification of fraternal incest, through which music, song, and miraculous life are born in the text, in earshot. Like perfume, music is the daughter of an incestuous passion. Like perfume, it's the volatile chiseled object inscribing, in brief motifs, the reasoning of a strange body, distracted by the power of jouissance.

Scheherazade's Night Becomes Possible

Scheherazade wakes up on the sand. The trembling dawn holds my scratched gaze in the air. Dawn awakens. In Scheherazade's form, the sea doubles the deployment of the light. A large bird escapes: Scheherazade lets any deviation from the tide spill over. Dawn and the large bird impregnate the sea: Scheherazade bathes, in free fall, while deserting the other end of the shore. She slides, slides, slides, up to the bird, up to the shock—my scratched gaze. The wind, in its speed, takes up a vapor of sunlight and perhaps incinerated, sleepy fish. I see, in a wink, the fish in the foam. Whiteness. Scene held still, O wave atop the line that is crossed then obliterated. And between the body and the foam, seeing and hearing, the foam—like a trembling of the stars—fixes my inundated face. It's a wave in mirror image, seen in the foam then burned into me: an ashen incision of your name.

Scheherazade throws off her clothes. The sand burns in the wind. Scheherazade is bathing. And perhaps the dress outlined in the sand will dig out a capricious variation of its own mirror image. Scheherazade is swimming. Dawn has arisen and goes toward her, like a circle in a circle. The foam's disappearance. The beating of the body. A gyratory frisson. The echo of the foam emits the being cut off from time.

ACKNOWLEDGMENTS

Friends helped me complete this text, either through drawings or through translation (A. Diouri translated the tale of "The Talking Bird"). This mutual tattooing, which need not occur within a special protocol, must nevertheless include, in exergue, the play of its own inscription.

TRANSLATOR'S ACKNOWLEDGMENTS

Thanks to the editors at *PMLA* for publishing an excerpt of "Tattoos: Writing in Dots," in *PMLA* 137, no. 2 (2022), as well as to Jane Hiddleston and Khalid Lyamlahy for including "The Text's Crystal" and an excerpt of "The Calligraphic Trace" in *Abdelkébir Khatibi: Postcolonialism, Transnationalism, and Culture in the Maghreb and Beyond* (Liverpool, England: Liverpool University Press, 2020). Thanks also to the Centre national du livre (CNL) for providing a translation grant to help finish this work. Thanks to Soufien Mestaoui, Hassan Massoudy, Brahim El Guabli, Khalid Lyamlahy, and Fatah Beddani for their valuable insights into some of the cultural materials discussed here. Thanks as well to the team at Northwestern University Press, most notably, Faith Wilson Stein, Mary Klein, and Maddie Schultz, and to Lily Sadowsky for her scrupulous copyediting. Thanks to Rajeev Kinra, Laura Brueck, and the committee for the Humanities in Translation Prize for selecting this work.

NOTES

Translator's Note

1. Tahar Ben Jelloun, "Décolonisation de la sociologie au Maghreb," *Le Monde diplomatique*, August 1974, 18. [Translator's note: All translations are mine.]

2. Zakya Daoud, "Abdelkebir Khatibi: Il faut s'essayer à une double critique permanente," *Lamalif* 57 (February 1973): 32–34. For an English version, see Zakya Daoud and Abdelkébir Khatibi, "We Must Attempt a Lasting Double Critique," trans. Matt Reeck, in *Lamalif: A Critical Anthology of Societal Debates in Morocco during the Years of Lead (1966–1988)*, ed. Brahim El Guabli and Ali Alalou (Liverpool, England: Liverpool University Press, 2023), 1:267–73.

3. Roman Jakobson, *Essais de linguistique générale*, trans. Nicolas Ruwet (Paris: Minuit, 1963), 86. For an English version, see Roman Jakobson, "On Linguistic Aspects of Translation," in *The Translation Studies Reader*, ed. Lawrence Venuti (London: Routledge, 2012), 126–31.

4. David Fieni, "Désappropriation de soi et poétique de l'intersigne chez Khatibi," *Expressions maghrébines* 12, no. 1 (2013): 1–17.

5. Matt Reeck, "Tattoos: Writing in Dots," *PMLA* 137, no. 2 (2022): 296.

6. Abdelkébir Khatibi, *Maghreb pluriel* (Paris: Denoël, 1983). For an English version, see Khatibi, *Plural Maghreb: Writings on Postcolonialism*, trans. P. Burçu Yalim (London: Bloomsbury, 2021).

7. Jacques Derrida, *Le Monolinguisme de l'autre* (Paris: Galilée, 1996). For an English version, see Derrida, *Monolinguism of the Other; or, The Prosthesis of Origin*, trans. Patrick Mensah (Palo Alto, CA: Stanford University Press, 1998).

8. One noteworthy recent example of decolonization theory and practice that takes Khatibi's lead is Mohamed Amer Meziane's *Au bord des mondes: Vers une anthropologie métaphysique* (Brussels: Vues de l'esprit, 2023).

Introduction

1. [Translator's note: Stéphane Mallarmé, "Notes sur le théâtre," *La Revue indépendante* 5, no. 2 (March 1887): 391, https://gallica.bnf.fr/ark:/12148/bpt6k1050702s/f89.item. Mallarmé wrote this column for *La Revue indépendante de littérature et d'art* from November 1886 to July 1887. The magazine was founded by Édouard Dujardin, and the editor-in-chief was Félix Fénéon.]

2. See the postface on the sign in Pierre Klossowski's *Les Lois de l'hospitalité* (Paris: Gallimard, 1965), 335. [Translator's note: "General delivery" refers to mail that is held at a post office because the recipient has no local address; the recipient is asked to come to the post office to collect the mail.]

3. Remember what Jean Starobinski said about the Saussurian anagram: "Poetic discourse will only be a name's second *way of being*." See Starobinski,

Les Mots sous les mots: Les anagrammes de Ferdinand de Saussure (Paris: Gallimard, 1971), 33.

4. I am thinking particularly of Julia Kristeva's *Sèméiotikè: Recherches pour une sémanlayse*, Tel Quel (Paris: Seuil, 1969).

5. [Translator's note: Khatibi does not indicate which verse of the Qur'an he is specifically thinking about. I cite two relevant passages: "For We have sent down clear messages to you and only those who defy [God] would refuse to believe them" (Qur'an 2:99) and "As for those who hide the proofs and guidance We send down, after We have made them clear to people in the Scripture, God rejects them, and so do others, unless they repent, make amends, and declare the truth" (2:159–60). All translations of the Qur'an are by M. A. S. Abdel Haleem (Oxford, England: Oxford University Press, 2004).]

6. [Translator's note: Qur'an 17:36.]

7. [Translator's note: Likely another reference to Qur'an 2:159–60.]

8. [Translator's note: Qur'an 18:10.]

9. [Translator's note: Qur'an 17:12.]

10. [Translator's note: Qur'an 6:97.]

Chapter 1

1. Roland Barthes, *Sade, Fourier, Loyola* (Paris: Seuil, 1971), 162. [Translator's note: The translation here is by Richard Miller. See Barthes, *Sade, Fourier, Loyola*, trans. Richard Miller (New York: Wang Hill, 1976), 158–59.]

2. [Translator's note: Khatibi does not cite his source, but it is Louis Massignon, "Réflexions sur la structure primitive de l'analyse grammaticale en arabe," in *Parole donnée*, intro. Vincent Monteil (Paris: Julliard, 1962), 331.]

3. [Translator's note: No citation.]

4. See the mystic Razi.

5. This note owes a lot to the remarkable Orientalist Louis Massignon, who wrote, "In order to understand the other, we must become their hosts, not subsume them into what we know. The 'exogamic' character of language is realizable only while using the right of asylum." See especially "Réflexions sur la structure primitive de l'analyse grammaticale en arabe" and "Voyelles sémitiques et sémantique musicale," both in *Parole donnée*, 327–41, 342–46.

6. "For the signifier is a unit in its very uniqueness, being by nature symbol only of an absence. Which is why we cannot say of the purloined letter that, like other objects, it must be *or* not be in a particular place but that unlike them it will be *and* not be where it is, wherever it goes." Jacques Lacan, "Le Séminaire sur 'La Lettre volée,'" in *Écrits* (Paris: Seuil, 1966), 24. [Translator's note: The translation is from Lacan, "Seminar on 'The Purloined Letter,'" trans. Jeffrey Mehlman, *Yale French Studies* 48 (1972), 54.]

7. [Translator's note: This is from the thirty-forth hadith in Abu Zakariyya Yahya ibn Sharaf al-Nawawi's collection of forty, *Al-Arba'ūn al-nawawiyyah*, https://sunnah.com/nawawi40:34.]

8. The numbering in parentheses corresponds to that of the corpus; see annexes II or III.

9. "My body is never reducible to the representation that I make of it, or of God. And if it comes about that humans find a way to adequately speak of their

body, the very notion of God will disappear." Denis Vasse, *Le Temps du désir* (Paris: Seuil, 1969), 19.

10. [Translator's note: No citation.]

11. [Translator's note: No citation.]

12. John Lyons, *Linguistique générale: Introduction à la linguistique théorique*, trans. Françoise Dubois-Charlier and David Robinson (Paris: Larousse, 1970), 137. [Translator's note: John Lyons, *Introduction to Theoretical Linguistics* (Cambridge, England: Cambridge University Press, 1969), 177.]

13. Algirdas Julien Greimas, "Les Proverbes et les dictons," in *Du sens: Essais sémiotiques* (Paris: Seuil, 1970), 310–11.

14. The importance of which we're just beginning to discover. See Jean Starobinski, *Les Mots sous les mots: Les anagrammes de Ferdinand de Saussure* (Paris: Gallimard, 1971).

15. Elli Köngäs Maranda, "Structure des énigmes," *L'Homme* 9, no. 3 (1969): 38.

16. This is, it seems, the function of another riddle-like discourse, so important to popular culture in our time: the crime novel. Although it's based on the narrative form of myths, this type of novel is, in actuality, only the expansion of a "monk's riddle."

17. Greimas, *Du sens*, 312.

18. George B. Milner, "De l'armature des locutions proverbiales: Essai de taxonomie sémantique," *L'Homme* 9, no. 3 (1969): 54.

19. [Translator's note: In Khatibi's text, this is initially rendered in the singular—*un cheveu*, or "a hair"—but in the annex, it's made plural. I'm imposing the plural variation here.]

20. [Translator's note: Khatibi again uses variations of the proverb in question. The French translation in the text contains "a bald woman" and "her comb and her hair," whereas the annex supplies a version containing "the bald woman" and "a comb and hair." In this case, I've used the text's translation and changed the annex to match it.]

21. [Translator's note: Massignon, no citation. Although it's not clear to which text Khatibi refers, it's likely the chapter "Comment ramener à une base commune l'étude de deux cultures: L'Arabe et la gréco-latine," in *Parole donnée*, 301–18.]

22. [Translator's note: Stéphane Mallarmé, "Le Tombeau d'Edgar Poe," in *Poésies*, 8th ed. (Paris: Nouvelle revue française, 1914), 131–32.]

23. [Translator's note: Qur'an 96:1.]

24. Derrida's grammatology allows the founding of the Lacanian debate and, through it, the measuring of the historical movement.

25. Friedrich Nietzsche, *Le Livre du philosophe: Études théorétiques*, trans. Angèle Kremer-Marietti (Paris: Flammarion, [1969] 1991), 80.

26. Jakobson, *Essais de linguistique générale*, 86. [Translator's note: Jakobson, "On Linguistic Aspects of Translation," 131.]

27. Walter Benjamin writes, "True translation is transparent, it does not obscure the original, does not stand in its light, but rather allows pure language, as if strengthened by its own medium, to shine even more fully on the original." Walter Benjamin, *Œuvres*, vol. 1, *Mythe et violence*, trans. Maurice de Gandillac (Paris: Denoël, 1971), 72. [Translator's note: The translation is from Benjamin, "The Translator's Task," trans. Steven Rendall, *TTR* 10, no. 2 (1997): 162.]

28. [Translator's note: Since Khatibi's chapter is based on the mnemonic device of mapping proverbs onto a body, he maintains explicit references to the body parts referred to in the Arabic proverbs. I have followed him. A translation that forgoes this literalness could be "The days of youth will be taken over by the days of motherhood."]

29. Arabic pornographers speak openly about the *tears* of sperm.

30. It seems that new themes don't betray the logical and musical character of the dialectal word. The privilege afforded to lexical combinatorics and rhythm is a timely and deliberate gesture on our part. Diachronic research allowed us to more clearly specify the transformations due to new themes.

31. Claude Lévi-Strauss, *Le Cru et le cuit* (Paris: Plon, 1964), 26. [Translator's note: This translation is that of John and Doreen Weightman. See *Introduction to a Science of Mythology*, vol. 1, *The Raw and the Cooked*, trans. John Weightman and Doreen Weightman (New York: Harper and Row, 1969), 18.]

32. [Translator's note: See Friedrich Nietzsche, *Thus Spoke Zarathustra*, trans. Thomas Common (New York: Modern Library, 1917), 89, 90, 113, 117, 219.]

33. [Translator's note: Khatibi directs the reader to the introduction of al-Jahiz's *Kitāb al-bukhalāʾ* but does not provide a citation. See Abou Othman Amr ibn Bahr al-Djahiz de Basra, *Le Livre des avares*, ed. Gerlof van Vloten (Leiden, the Netherlands: Brill, 1900); or, for an English version, al-Jāḥiẓ, *The Book of Misers: Al-Bukhalāʾ*, trans. Robert Bertram Serjeant (Reading, England: Garnet, 2000).]

34. Georges Bataille, *Sur Nietzsche* (Paris: Gallimard, 1967), 92.

Chapter 2

1. See Jacques Derrida, *De la grammatologie* (Paris: Minuit, 1967) and Jacques Derrida, "Sémiologie et grammatologie," *Social Science Information* 7, no. 3 (1968): 133–48. See also François Wahl, "La Structure, le sujet, la trace, ou De deux philosophies au-delà du structuralisme: Jacques Lacan et Jacques Derrida," in *Qu'est-ce que le structuralisme?* (Paris: Seuil, 1968), 390–441.

2. See also the different approach in Roland Barthes's beautiful book, *L'Empire des signes (le Japon)* (Geneva: Skira, 1970).

3. This is essentially what the linguist Emilio Alarcos Llorach says in a subsection of the chapter "Communication graphique" in the Encyclopédie de la Pléiade volume on language. See Emilio Alarcos Llorach, "Les Graphèmes du point de vue graphématique," in *Le Langage*, ed. André Martinet (Paris: Gallimard, 1968), 551–52.

4. Joseph Herber, "Notes sur les tatouages au Maroc," *Hespéris* 36 (1949): 46.

5. [Translator's note: All biblical translations are from the New International Version.]

6. James George Frazer, *Le Folklore de l'Ancien Testament*, trans. Émile Audra (Paris: P. Geuthner, 1924), 64–65.

7. Notice that this sign is found among Moroccan Jews, who tattoo the foreheads of babies in this fashion. We also know that, in Islam, the forehead is the place of thought: "You can see the hostility on the faces of the disbelievers when Our messages are recited clearly to them" (Qurʾan 22:72). According to Islamic tradition, the Antichrist will come with a sign on his forehead: KFR (kafr).

8. Exodus 13:9.

9. Revelation 7:2–8.
10. Revelation 19:16.
11. Exodus 20:4.
12. [Translator's note: Cesare Lombroso, "The Savage Origin of Tattooing," *Popular Science Monthly* 48 (April 1896): 802.]
13. [Translator's note: Muhammad ibn ʿIsa al-Tirmidhi, *Jāmiʿ al-Tirmidhī*, vol. 5, bk. 41, *Kitāb al-adab*, hadith 2782, https://sunnah.com/tirmidhi:2782.]
14. The bismillah is a primordial Qurʾanic phrase: "In the name of God, the Most Gracious, the Most Merciful."
15. [Translator's note: No citation, apocryphal reference.]
16. One book dedicated to Arab painting, Richard Ettinghausen's *La Peinture arabe*, trans. Yves Rivière (Geneva: Skira, 1962), skirts this movement; it affords an undue importance to the art of miniatures, which is a minor art in Arab culture. This art allows the West to conceal difference.
17. [Translator's note: Without giving a particular citation, Khatibi refers to Herodotus, who discusses tattoos in several places in *The Histories*.]
18. [Translator's note: Ibn Manzur, *Lisān al-ʿarab* (n.p., 1290).]
19. At least that is what Maurice Gaudefroy-Demombynes speculates. See Gaudefroy-Demombynes, *Les Institutions musulmanes* (Paris: Flammarion, 1953), 59–60.
20. Hamid Bénani settled on this very word for the title of his film, although he had originally chosen the word *stigmates*. In the final cut, he opted for *Wechma*, with *Traces* as the subtitle. This lexical tripolarity is apparent at the level of the film's combinatorics. [Translator's note: This film from 1970 was reformatted for DVD in 2012 and distributed by Paris Ouagadougou Montréal (POM) Films. The film is no longer listed on POM Films' website.]
21. [Translator's note: Khatibi is referring to his experimental autobiographical novel *La Mémoire tatouée* (Paris: Denoël, 1971), whose title literally means "tattooed memory."]
22. Aesthetic paleontology teaches us a lesson in modesty. See André Leroi-Gourhan, *Le Geste et la parole*, 2 vols. (Paris: Albin Michel, 1964–65).
23. Stéphane Mallarmé, *Crayonné au théâtre*, in *Œuvres completes* (Paris: Gallimard, 1945), 304. [Translator's note: The translation is from Mallarmé, *Divagations*, trans. Barbara Johnson (Cambridge, MA: Harvard University Press, 2007), 130.]
24. See James Germain Février, *Histoire de l'écriture* (Paris: Payot, 1948), 18.
25. Derrida's work is crucial for the entirety of this debate.
26. Février, *Histoire*, 17.
27. Ideography: writing in words. Ideography is different from pictography, which is composed of successive elements linked to "real" objects or to symbols.
28. Février, *Histoire*, 30–31.
29. Claude Levi-Strauss, *Le Totémisme aujourd'hui* (Paris: Presses universitaires de France, 1962).
30. Umberto Eco, "Sémiologie des messages visuels," *Communications* 15 (1970): 50.
31. André Leroi-Gourhan writes about decoration, "It's not impossible to think that a study of Paleolithic art oriented in a certain way would introduce surprising new facts into linguistic consideration." See Leroi-Gourhan, *Le Geste*, 246.

32. Turning from one line to another, like oxen from one furrow to another.

33. Jacques Derrida, *De la grammatologie*, 408. [Translator's note: I have used Gayatri Chakravorty Spivak's translation. See Derrida, *Of Grammatology*, trans. Gayatri Chakravorty Spivak (Baltimore: Johns Hopkins University Press, 1976), 288.]

34. Qur'an 2:223.

35. [Translator's note: The hadith speaks of a child born cross-eyed, not with one eye. See Tirmidhi, *Jāmiʿ*, vol. 5, bk. 44, *Kitāb al-tafsīr*, hadith 2978, https://sunnah.com/tirmidhi:2978.]

36. Speaking broadly, the face is covered with a cloth veil or simply with a hand to the mouth.

37. See chapter 5.

38. Anaphorically, *oë* means the eye *in* the eye.

39. Called the "hand of Fatima," a nonsensical phrase, in the vulgate as well as the imperial lingo. It isn't the sense of owning that defines the pentagram but its vacuity and its migration as a sign.

40. Julia Kristeva, "Le Geste: Pratique ou communication?" *Langages* 3, no. 10 (1968): 51.

41. See Joseph Herbert, "La Main de Fathma," *Hespéris* 7 (1927); and, more importantly, Dominique Champault and A. R. Verbrugge, *La Main: Ses figurations au Maghreb et au Levant* (Paris: Catalogue du musée de l'Homme, 1965).

42. This verticality is attested to in radical ways by the painter Mohamed Melehi:

> I reduced the collage to the essential: *verticality and the color black*. In black, I found the void and calmness. In verticality, the rhythm of the human. For me, everything vertical is living. Rain falls vertically, we pray vertically, the number one is vertical. Plants grow from the ground vertically. One vertical band next to another signifies order, succession, and continuity. It's this order that I saw missing in the world created by humans and that I projected into my collages.

See Mohamed Melehi, *Souffles* 7–8 (1967): 58.

43. See Derrida's rigorous and admirable analysis of the hymen in Mallarmé's writing, "La Double séance," in *La Dissémination* (Paris: Seuil, 1972). [Translator's note: "La Double séance," or "The Double Session" in Barbara Johnson's translation, is the second of the book's three parts. For an English translation, see Derrida, *Dissemination*, trans. Barbara Johnson (Chicago: University of Chicago Press, 1981), 173–286.]

44. Champault and Verbrugge, *La Main*, n.p.

45. "Each of our card-designs corresponds to a twofold necessity and must assume a double function. It must be an independent object, and it must serve for the dialogue—or the duel—in which two partners meet face to face. It must also play the role which is assigned to each card, in its capacity as a member of the pack, in the game as a whole. Its vocation is a complicated one, therefore: and it must satisfy demands of more than one sort—symmetrical, where its functions are concerned, asymmetrical where its role is in question. The problem is solved by the use of a design which is symmetrical but yet lies across an oblique axis. (An entirely asymmetrical design would have sufficed for the role but not for the

function; and vice versa in the case of a design that was wholly symmetrical.) Once again we have a complicated situation based upon two contradictory forms of duality, and resulting in a compromise brought about by a secondary opposition between the ideal axis of the object itself and the ideal axis of the figure which it represents." Claude Lévi-Strauss, *Tristes tropiques* (Paris: Plon, 1955), 199. [Translator's note: This translation is by John Russell. See Lévi-Strauss, *Tristes tropiques*, trans. John Russell (London: Criterion, 1961), 176.]

46. Truco is a Spanish game similar to tarot cards. See Jorge Luis Borges, *Evaristo Carriego*, trans. François-Marie Rosset (Paris: Seuil, 1969). [Translator's note: Khatibi provides an incomplete citation to a French translation of Jorge Luis Borges's biography of the Argentine musician Evaristo Carriego.]

47. I prefer this expression over the catch-all *communication.*

48. Lévi-Strauss, *Tristes Tropiques*, 201.

49. Derrida, *La Dissémination*, 241. [Translator's note: This passage appears on pp. 212–13 of Johnson's translation.]

50. See part 5.

51. See the analysis of color and its triple register in Julia Kristeva, "L'Espace de Giotto," *Peinture: Cahiers théoriques* 2/3 (1972): 35–51.

52. [Translator's note: No reference. Syphilis was first detected in Italy after the French invasion of Naples in 1494–1495.]

53. Aline Réveillaud de Lens, *Pratiques des harems marocains* (Paris: Geuthner, 1925), 79.

54. The practice of cautery is still active in Morocco, where hot needles are applied to babies to conjure and expel "bad blood." The procedure is as follows, according to one witness: After making the baby swallow a carefully prepared medicine (each *farâga* seems to have her own concoction), the farâga makes incisions around the stomach, under the belly button, with a kitchen knife. Using a bit of wood, she applies hot needles to different parts of the body. "Bad blood" seems to refer, generally, to transmissible diseases, like syphilis, called by the pretty name of *flowers*. The symbolic efficacy of such medicine remains little studied in Morocco.

55. Attestation reported by Joseph Herber, "Tatouages curatifs au Maroc," *Revue d'ethnographie et des traditions populaires* 34–36 (1928): 179–87.

56. Jean Lacassagne and Joseph Herber, *Du tatouage chez les prostituées en Afrique du Nord* (Paris: J. Desvigne, 1935), 5.

57. [Translator's note: Herber uses the word "joyeux" in scare quotes. This indicates a soldier in the light infantry battalions in North Africa, known as "Bat' d'Af'" or BILA (bataillons d'infanterie légère d'Afrique). These disciplinary units were composed of convicts from metropolitan France and soldiers in North Africa who were being punished for malfeasances. See the military entry under "Joyeux," Centre National de Ressources Textuelles et Lexicales, 2012, https://www.cnrtl.fr/definition/joyeux. See also the Wikipedia page for the BILA at https://en.wikipedia.org/wiki/Battalions_of_Light_Infantry_of_Africa.]

58. Joseph Herber, *Les Tatouages des prostituées marocaines* (Paris: Ernest Leroux, 1919).

59. How is self-tattooing possible? The technique is relatively simple. But it relies on a mythic discourse: recall the Moroccan rite for the apprentice tattoo artist, which begins with offerings to the marabout protector-saint. That night,

the apprentice dreams that the saintly man offers her a needle. We have done the same thing in writing this text. But who will know?

60. Nietzsche, *Thus Spoke Zarathustra*, 118.

61. [Translator's note: No reference.]

62. [Translator's note: Paul Klee, no citation.]

63. Joseph Herbert, "Onomastique des tatouages marocains," *Hespéris* 35 (1948): 31–56.

64. Stéphane Mallarmé, "Ballets," in *Divagations* (Paris: Eugène Fasquelle, 1897), 175. [Translator's note: This is Barbara Johnson's translation. See Mallarmé, *Divigations*, trans. Johnson, 129.]

65. A more complete list can be found in Herber's article. This list is *suggestive*.

66. Roman Jakobson, "Sur l'art verbal de William Blake et d'autres peintres-poètes," in *Hypothèses: Trois entretiens et trois études sur la linguistique et la poétique*, ed. Noam Chomsky, Roman Jakobson, and Morris Halle, trans. Jean-Pierre Faye (Paris: Seghers/Laffont, 1972), 82. The reduction of rhetoric to two poles (metaphor and metonymy) reaffirms metaphysical binarism and frames analysis in a logocentric place. See Derrida's critique in *De la grammatologie*. [Translator's note: Jakobson is quoting a previous text. See Roman Jakobson, "Poetry of Grammar and Grammar of Poetry," *Lingua* 21 (1968).]

Chapter 3

1. Barthes, *Sade, Fourier, Loyola*, 162. [Translator's note: The translation here is again by Richard Miller, 158–59.]

2. [Translator's note: Although Khatibi does not specifically refer to it, the book he's drawing from is Georges Bataille's *L'Érotisme* (Paris: Minuit, 1957). For an English version, see *Eroticism: Death and Sensuality*, trans. Mary Dalwood (San Francisco: City Lights, 1986).]

3. [Translator's note: Khatibi quotes from Nafzawi's introduction to the text. but the citation might be partially misused. In Nafzawi's text, this sentence follows a statement in which the author "bears witness" (*témoigne*) to the fact that "there is no God but Allah" and that "He has nothing to do with this book." See Cheikh Nefzaoui, *Le Jardin parfumé: Manuel d'érotologie arabe*, trans. [Redacted] (Paris: Isidore Liseux, 1886; repr., 1910), 12, https://babel.hathitrust.org/cgi/pt?id=njp.32101005926405&view=1up&seq=13. Two other French versions exist. See Cheikh Nefzaoui, *Le Parfum des prairies (le jardin parfumé): Manuel d'érotologie arabe*, trans. Antonin Terme and the Moor Nefissah (n.p., 1860; repr., Paris: Jean Fort, 1935), https://gallica.bnf.fr/ark:/12148/bpt6k854677v/f9.image#; and Mohammed El Nefzaoui, *Le Jardin parfumé: Manuel d'érotologie arabe*, trans. [Redacted], ed. Yasser Ali (n.p.: Minerve, 1991), https://archive.org/details/lejardinparfumem0000elne/page/n5/mode/2up.]

4. [Translator's note: The first translation of Nafzawi's book into European languages was this 1876 translation into French by a military officer whose full name is elided. It remains for all intents and purposes anonymous.]

5. [Translator's note: This "translator's note" is not mine; it exists in the French text and is likely that of one of the three anonymous translators.]

6. [Translator's note: Evidently, fifty plus ten doesn't equal seventy, despite the text saying so.]

7. See Marcel Détienne's beautiful book, to which we owe many of our aromatic allusions, *Les Jardins d'Adonis*, intro. Jean-Pierre Vernant (Paris: Gallimard, 1972).

8. [Translator's note: No citation.]

9. [Translator's note: Sophocles, no citation.]

10. Détienne, *Les Jardins d'Adonis*, 122–25.

11. Stéphane Mallarmé, *Œuvres complètes*, 309. [Translator's note: The phrase in Mallarmé is "la Danseuse [semble] la mouvante écume suprême"; in Barbara Johnson's translation, the "Dancer [seems] the topmost moving foam." This appears in the context of a spectator being transported by the classical music accompanying a ballet; the dancer is a final articulation of this musical and physical energy. See Stéphane Mallarmé, "Notes sur le théâtre," *La Revue indépendante* 3, no. 2 (January 1887): 59; Mallarmé, "Parenthesis," in *Divagations*, trans. Johnson, 153.]

12. [Translator's note: Charles Baudelaire, "Correspondences," in *Selected Poems of Charles Baudelaire*, trans. Geoffrey Wagner (New York: Grove, 1946), n.p.]

13. "To do this he had first had to master the grammar, to understand the syntax of smells, to get a firm grasp on the rules that govern them, and once he was familiar with their dialect . . . to analyse the construction of their sentences, to weigh the proportion of their words, to measure the arrangement of their periods." Then further on: "[The] history [of perfume making] followed, that of the French language step by step." Joris-Karl Huysmans, *À rebours* (Paris: Fasquelle, 1955), 151–52. [Translator's note: This translation is from the Penguin Classics edition, translated by Robert Baldick. See Huysmans, *Against Nature* (New York: Penguin, 1959), 120.]

14. Spirits, essences: two metaphysical terms.

15. The elephant sura from the Qur'an is as follows: "In the name of God, the Lord of Mercy, Do you [Prophet] not see how your Lord dealt with the army of the elephant? Did He not utterly confound their plans? He sent flocks of birds against them, pelting them with pellets of hard-baked clay: He made them [like] cropped stubble." [Translator's note: Qur'an 105:1–5.]

16. [Translator's note: No citation is given for Nafzawi's retelling of the story of Musaylima, who, despite being called Musaylima ibn Qays here, is typically referred to as Musaylima ibn Ḥabīb. See https://en.wikipedia.org/wiki/Musaylima.]

17. [Translator's note: Khatibi doesn't provide her full name, which is Sajah bint al-Harith ibn Suwayd al-Tamimi. See https://en.wikipedia.org/wiki/Sajah.]

18. [Translator's note: Khatibi does not provide a citation, but these are episodes from *Le Jardin parfumé*. See Nefzaoui, *Le Jardin parfumé* (Paris: Isidore Liseux, 1886; repr., 1910), 24–39, 43–67, https://babel.hathitrust.org/cgi/pt?id=njp.32101005926403&view=1up&seq=13.]

19. [Translator's note: Khatibi does not cite these quotations, but they are from *Le Jardin parfumé*. See pages 122, 121, and 34 of the Isidore Liseux edition, to which all subsequent citations refer. Interestingly, the first is slightly misquoted, as the saying is presented as a couplet (as I've indicated here). Also, the third citation reads as follows in Khatibi's text: "Son vagin semble absorber la verge

et fait croire qu'elle le suce comme tète le jeune enfant le sein de sa mère" (167). Yet this is a subtle miscitation of the original French translation, "Et l'attraction de sa vulve semblait pomper le membre, comme si elle le suçait, de la même sorte qu'un petit enfant tette le sein de sa mère" (34). Perhaps the most noteworthy difference is the alternation of *vagina* and *vulva* as practically synonymous terms. I'm repairing Khatibi's text to reflect the original French.]

20. [Translator's note: Bataille, *L'Érotisme*, 79.]

21. [Translator's note: No citation.]

22. [Translator's note: Nefzaoui, *Le Jardin parfumé*, 32.]

23. [Translator's note: Khatibi miscites the original French translation, transforming a "sword" into "sands." I've corrected the text. Nefzaoui, *Le Jardin parfumé*, 35.]

24. [Translator's note: Nefzaoui, *Le Jardin parfumé*, 5.]

25. [Translator's note: Nefzaoui, *Le Jardin parfumé*, 35–36.]

26. We know that Freud was largely convinced by the Oriental interpretation of dreams.

27. [Translator's note: Ibn Khaldun, no citation.]

28. [Translator's note: See Abu 'Abdallah Muhammad al-Bukhari, *Ṣaḥīḥ al-Bukhārī*, vol. 9, bk. 87, *Kitāb al-ta'bīr*, hadith 144, https://sunnah.com/bukhar i:7017.]

Chapter 4

Epigraphs: [Translator's note: Although he doesn't cite his soure, Khatibi seems to be using the French translation by Vincent Monteil: "Car le Coran est un livre redoutable qui rappelle à l'homme la mémoire de la mort et de l'au-delà. Il ne doit pas être un prétexte à faire de la belle musique." See Ibn Khaldun, *Discours sur l'histoire universelle: Al-Muqaddima*, trans. Vincent Monteil (Beirut: Commission internationale pour la traduction des chefs-d'œuvre, 1967), n.p. My English translation here is based, however, on the first French translation, that of the Irish-born French national William McGuckin de Slane: "En effet, la lecture du Coran est faite pour inspirer l'effroi, parce qu'elle dirige nos pensées vers la morte et ce qui s'en suit; elle ne doit pas servir à procurer du plaisir aux personnes qui recherchent la perception de sons agréables." *Les Prolégomènes d'Ibn Khaldoun*, vol. 2, trans. de Slane (Paris: Imprimerie impériale, 1865), 416. This passage was not included in the abridged English translation by Franz Rosenthal, *The Muqaddimah: An Introduction to History; The Classic Islamic History of the World* (Princeton, NJ: Princeton University Press, 1967).]
[Translator's note: Friedrich Nietzsche, *Thus Spoke Zarathustra*, 243.]

1. See Derrida, *De la grammatologie*, 52.

2. [Translator's note: Khatibi appears to be citing from memory. The full citation in Rosenthal's English translation is as follows: "Our *shaykh*, the sharîf Judge Abû l-Qâsim as-Sabtî, who was the chief cultivator of the Arabic language in his time, used to say: 'The different kinds of rhetorical figures may occur to a poet or a secretary, but it is ugly if he uses many of them. They belong among the things that embellish speech and constitute its beauty. They are like moles on a face. One or two make it beautiful, but many make it ugly' " (Ibn Khaldun, *The Muqaddimah*, 455).]

3. Ahmad al-Qalqashandi, *Ṣubḥ al-aʿshā*, vol. 3 (Cairo: Al-Matbaʿah al-amiriyah, 1914), n.p. [Translator's note: See also Heba El-Toudy and Tarek Galal Abdelhamid, eds., *Selections from "Ṣubḥ al-aʿshā" by al-Qalqashandī, Clerk of the Mamluk Court: Egypt; "Seats of Government" and "Regulations of the Kingdom," from Early Islam to the Mamluks* (London: Routledge, 2017).]

4. Al-Qalqashandi, *Ṣubḥ al-aʿshā*, n.p.

5. [Translator's note: Muslim ibn Hajjaj al-Naysaburi, *Saḥīḥ Muslim*, bk. 4, *Kitāb al-masājid*, hadith 1062, https://sunnah.com/muslim:523a.]

6. Qurʾan 13:39.

7. The state before birth: no relation at all to metempsychosis.

8. Seyyed Moussa Sadr, "Les Fawâtih ou lettres séparées," *Les Cahiers de l'Oronte* (Beirut: Société d'impression et d'édition libanaise, 1966), 31.

9. Louis Massignon, *Opera minora*, vol. 2 (Paris: Presses universitaires de France, 1969), 554.

10. Among Buddhist scribes and monks, we find the same mystical asceticism with respect to the calligraphic trace: "Thus a certain Buddhist monk, isolated for thirty years at the top of a pavilion, made this his sole occupation." See "L'Écriture chinoise," in *L'Écriture et la psychologie des peuples* (Paris: A. Colin, 1963). [Translator's note: Khatibi probably refers here to Jacques Gernet's "La Chine: Aspects et fonctions de l'écriture," in *L'Écriture et la psychologie des peoples* (Paris: Armand Colin, 1963), 29–49.]

11. Al-Qalqashandi, *Ṣubḥ al-aʿshā*, n.p.

12. In *Al-ʿIqd al-farîd*. [Translator's note: Khatibi refers here to Ibn 'Abd Rabbih's *Al-ʿIqd al-farīd*. Ibn 'Abd Rabbih (860–940) was an Arabic-language writer in Cordóba, Spain. The translation here is from *The Unique Necklace*, vol. 2, trans. Issa J. Boullata (Reading, England: Garnet Publishing, 2009), 1.]

13. *Al-Bayân wat-tabyyîn*. [Translator's note: Khatibi refers here to al-Jahiz's *Al-Bayân wa al-tabyīn* (*The Book of Eloquence and Oratory*). Al-Jahiz (c. 776–868) was a prolific Arabic writer from Basra said to be the author of 140 titles. No page number is listed for this citation and no English-language translation exists.]

14. Al-Jahiz, *Al-Bayân*, n.p.

15. Ibn Khaldun, *Discours sur l'histoire universelle*, trans. Vincent Monteil, n.p.

16. Lévi-Strauss, *Le Cru et le cuit*, 29. [Translator's note: The translation is from *The Raw and the Cooked*, trans. Weightman and Weightman, 21.]

17. Jakobson, "Sur l'art verbal de William Blake," 82.

18. Massignon, "Voyelles sémitiques et sémantique musicale," 343, 344.

19. Ibn Khaldun, *Discours sur l'histoire universelle*, trans. Vincent Monteil. [Translator's note: I have bridge translated from Monteil's French. For an annotated direct translation from Arabic, see David James, "The Commentaries of Ibn al-Baṣıṣ and Ibn al-Waḥīd on Ibn al-Bawwāb's 'Ode on the Art of Calligraphy' (*Raʾiyyah fīl-khaṭṭ*)," in *Back to the Sources: Biblical and Near Eastern Studies in Honour of Dermot Ryan*, ed. Kevin Cathcart and John Healey (Sandycove, Ireland: Glendale Press, 1989), 167–77.]

20. Erwin Panofsky, *L'Œuvre d'art et ses significations* (Paris: Gallimard, 1969), 76, 85n63.

21. In *L'Écriture et la psychologie des peuples* (Paris: A. Colin, 1963).

22. [Translator's note: Khatibi doesn't provide a citation, but the phrase can be found in Louis Massignon, *Écrits mémorables*, vol. 2 (Paris: Robert Laffont, 2009), 215.]

23. Naji Zain al-Din, *Atlas of Arabic Calligraphy* (Baghdad: Government Printing Department, 1968). [Translator's note: The Iraqi government simultaneously published an English translation and an Arabic version. See also Naji Zain al-Din, *Muṣawwar al-ḫaṭṭ al-ʿarabī* (Baghdad: Government Printing Department, 1968); as well as Naji Zain al-Din, *Badāʾiʾ al-khaṭṭ al-ʿarabī* (Baghdad: Mudriyat al-thaqafah al-ʿammah, 1972).]

24. Roger Caillois, "Les Thèmes fondamentaux de J. L. Borges," in *Jorge Luis Borges: Des témoins, correspondance, inédits, interférences, situations, essais, "Borges et Borges," chronologie de l'utraïsme, biographie, glossaire argentin, bibliographie, iconographie* (Paris: L'Herne, 1964), 214.

25. Qurʾan 2:255. [Translator's note: This example of the ayat al-kursi designed in a Kufic labyrinth is a copy of the calligraphy in the Mosque of Sultan al-Muʾayyad in Cairo by the famous Egyptian calligrapher Yousuf Ahmed (1869–1942).]

26. [Translator's note: This seal celebrates the rule of the Ottoman Albanian governor and de facto ruler of Egypt from 1805 to 1848. Like the Kufic labyrinth before it (figure 4.2), this was composed by the Egyptian calligrapher Yousuf Ahmed.]

27. [Translator's note: Khatibi cites "a prayer" as the meaning behind this calligraphy's text. It proves to be a prayerful quatrain from an ode by Ibn Sina: "O God, / Nothing is able to describe you / Forgive us, for we are humans / We did not truly know you." See https://diwandb.com/poem/كتفرعمب-ىرولا-ماصتعا .html. The final two lines, which are a general formula of supplication, read: "The most devoted of all the devotees said, 'We haven't worshipped You as You deserve to be worshipped.'" Also, it bears noting that this image was originally reproduced upside down in the French book.]

28. [Translator's note: Qurʾan 9:18.]

29. [Translator's note: Qurʾan 1:1.]

30. [Translator's note: Qurʾan 63:8. The description of the calligraphy is my own, and it extensively revises Khatibi's description, which is unclear and confusing.]

31. [Translator's note: This example is housed in Ulu Jami, the Grand Mosque of Bursa, Turkey.]

Chapter 5

[Translator's note: Khatibi published a large illustrated book on the subject of Arabic calligraphy the same year that this book was published. It was coedited by Mohammed Sijelmassi. Evidently, Khatibi was responsible for the text, and Sijelmassi for the images. See Khatibi and Sijelmassi, eds., *L'Art de la calligraphie arabe* (Vanves, France: Chêne, 1976). The history of this book is, however, interesting. That same year, it was translated into English by James Hughes under the title *The Splendor of Islamic Calligraphy* and published by Thames and Hudson in London. The following year, it was published in the United States by Rizzoli. A second edition of the French book was published by Gallimard in 1994. A revised and expanded version of the book was published in English by Thames and Hudson in 1996.]

1. [Translator's note: Khatibi is quoting from the first chapter of Lao Tzu's *Tao Te Ching*. At the time of Khatibi's writing, there was only one French translation available, that of Léon Wieger (1913), and the phrase that Khatibi cites in French as "obscurcir l'obscurité" (to obscure the obscure) is not found in Wieger's translation. A similar phrase, "mystère des mystères" (mystery of mysteries), is (http://www.taichi-kungfu.fr/tai-chi-kungfu-lyon/le-lao-tseu-tao-te-king-le-livre-de-la-voie-et-la-vertu-trad-leon-wieger/). The *Tao Te Ching* is famous for its polysemy, and the translation website "Bureau of Public Secrets" has compiled 175 English-language translations of the first chapter of the *Tao Te Ching*, none of which renders the phrase as Khatibi has done it in French (https://www.bopsecrets.org/gateway/passages/tao-te-ching.htm). Yet, Khatibi cites the *Tao Te Ching* for one express purpose: to point to a nonrational modus operandi for "explaining" how "The Talking Bird" works as a story. (An explanation is assumed to be rational by definition, hence the scare quotes around *explaining*.) The reference to Taoism is potentially helpful to Khatibi's justification of his method because the Tao is defined by two fundamental doctrines: first, that it exists beyond language and so any explanation (in language) can only fail to explain the true Tao; and, second, that the principles of being and nonbeing—variously called "obscurities," "mysteries," "abysses," "profundities," "dissolutions," etc.—are united in a space beyond comprehension. Unique to Khatibi's French translation is that the first character (*hsüan*, meaning "dark" or "mysterious," in Chinese) is rendered as an infinitive verb and not a noun or adjective. Here, I cite the *Encyclopaedia Britannica* entry for "hsüan":

> **hsüan**, common term in most forms of Chinese religion and philosophy that connotes a hidden or occult dimension to some aspect of experience or reality. First used metaphysically in the *Tao-te ching*, it is an idea that is given mystical significance in many aspects of later Taoist and Buddhist tradition. (last modified June 18, 2009, https://www.britannica.com/topic/hsuan)]

2. Benjamin, *Œuvres*, vol. 2, *Poésie et révolution*, trans. Maurice de Gandillac, Les Lettres nouvelles (Paris: Denoël, 1972), 146. [Translator's note: The English translation is from Benjamin, "The Storyteller: Reflections on the Works of Nikolai Leskov," in *Illuminations: Essays and Reflections*, ed. Hannah Arendt, trans. Harry Zohn (New York: Schocken Books, 1969), 89.]

3. [Translator's note: In this chapter, Khatibi casts a skein of interrelated words—*récit*, *conte*, and *texte*. The latter two words are innocuous in English translation: "fairy tale" (or just "tale") and "text." The first word carries some interesting ambiguity. I consistently translate it as "story," although this is first and foremost in the context of the chapter's title, "The Storyteller's Voice." This means that "story" in this sense carries the connotation of the oral tradition. For another way of understanding the word *récit* as a literary form, see Fredric Jameson's *The Antinomies of Realism* (London: Verso, 2013), which poses it against the *roman* (novel) in the French tradition. In this case, a story carries a teleological sense in that it traces the destiny of a central hero, whereas a novel is a capacious container in which affect unrelated to the hero's destiny becomes,

in the nineteenth and early twentieth centuries, increasingly central to the form's art.]

4. [Translator's note: The French Orientalist Antoine Galland (1646–1715) produced the first European translation of *One Thousand and One Nights*. It was first published in twelve volumes, from 1704 to 1717, under the title *Les Mille et une nuits: Contes arabes*. It was printed in The Hauge by Pierre Husson. For more information, please consult https://gallica.bnf.fr/essentiels/galland/mille-nuits.]

5. Antoine Galland, trans., *Les Mille et une nuits: Contes arabes*, vol. 3 (Paris: Garnier-Flammarion, 1965).

6. [Translator's note: Stéphane Mallarmé, preface to the 1897 edition of *Un coup de dés jamais n'abolira le hazard* (Paris: Nouvelle revue française, 1914). This translation is by A. S. Kline. See Mallarmé, *Un coup de dés jamais n'abolira le hasard* (*A Throw of the Dice Will Never Abolish Chance*), trans. A. S. Kline (Poetry in Translation, 2007), https://www.poetryintranslation.com/PITBR/French/MallarmeUnCoupdeDes.php.]

7. Klossowski, *Les Lois*, 337.

8. [Translator's note: *One Thousand and One Nights*, no citation.]

9. [Translator's note: Mallarmé, "Notes sur le théâtre," *La Revue indépendante* 5, no. 2 (March 1887): 391.]

10. [Translator's note: Bloch, no citation.]

11. [Translator's note: Barthes, no citation.]

12. Pierre Commelin, *Mythologie grecque et romaine* (Paris: Garnier, 1960), 145.